The Law of
Large Numbers

The Law of Large Numbers

How to Make Success Inevitable

Dr. Gary S. Goodman

Published 2019 by Gildan Media LLC
aka G&D Media
www.GandDmedia.com

THE LAW OF LARGE NUMBERS. Copyright © 2019 by Dr. Gary S. Goodman. All rights reserved.

No part of this book may be used, reproduced or transmitted in any manner whatsoever, by any means (electronic, photocopying, recording, or otherwise), without the prior written permission of the author, except in the case of brief quotations embodied in critical articles and reviews. No liability is assumed with respect to the use of the information contained within. Although every precaution has been taken, the author and publisher assume no liability for errors or omissions. Neither is any liability assumed for damages resulting from the use of the information contained herein.

Front Cover design by David Rheinhardt of Pyrographx

Interior design by Meghan Day Healey of Story Horse, LLC

Library of Congress Cataloging-in-Publication Data is available upon request

ISBN: 978-1-7225-0193-8

10   9   8   7   6   5   4   3   2   1

Contents

Afterword   129

Why You Need
to Read This Book

Are you achieving everything you want in life? Are you living up to your potential?

If not, this book is for you. It will help you to move from scarcity to abundance in your career and personal life. You'll see how success can be yours when you apply one simple principle: the Law of Large Numbers.

Examine the lives of the rich, the famous, and the great, and you'll see how they put the Law to work.

Lincoln lost almost every bid for elective office before he rose to the presidency. Edison failed to perfect the light bulb in thousands of experiments before succeeding. Bill Gates and other pioneers figured out how to democratize computing, empowering millions of people. The list goes on and on.

All of these people figured out the secret of success. It can be summarized in these words: *Do more.*

Do enough of anything and you'll succeed. Do more than that, and you'll grow rich. Do even more still, and you'll become a legend.

Everyday people win with this principle without knowing its name or its pervasiveness. The founder of an electronics firm stated, "I don't know any problem in business that a few more sales can't help."

The young athlete who doesn't get enough playing time in the team's games, takes extra fielding and batting practice every chance he gets. He doesn't stop until the sheer quantity of his efforts makes him a qualitatively better ballplayer.

The best employees are often those who come in early, stay late, and try to accomplish just one more thing every day than others do. Over the course of a career, these steady extra efforts pay off in promotions, raises, and disproportionate incomes.

What prevents more people from consistently using this principle? Often they're deluded into thinking that success stems from talent, or knowledge, or credentials, or even luck.

But as one person remarked, "The harder I work, the luckier I get!"

The more we do, the better we get. The more stimulated we are. The more we are informed by lots of experiences and data that trigger innovations. You may have heard this expression:

"If you want to get something done, give the assignment to a busy person!"

This seems illogical at first. If someone is busy, then he's probably too busy, right? And if someone isn't busy enough, then surely he can get it done.

But we know that the busier you are, and the more you're doing, the more capable you are of doing still more. Like a muscle, your capacity increases when it is stretched. When it isn't stretched, you can only lift less and less. This is the reason those who aren't challenged are least likely to bear the load when called upon.

The purpose of my books has always been to help people to help themselves. I've helped them to sell, to perform customer service, to become independent consultants, and even to become better parents and coaches.

But I've never written a book that I could honestly say is for everyone.

The Law of Large Numbers is just that. It expresses a universal principle. It is so basic, so encompassing, that I've found that it works in every significant area of life.

You can use it to increase sales and build your business. You can make it the centerpiece of your diet and fitness plan. You can just as readily use it to develop a robust and exciting social life, brimming with friends and intimates.

In fact, try as I might, I have not found an area to which it *doesn't* apply.

And this excites me, because it is like the air we breathe. It is pervasive and essential, yet mostly overlooked, except when it is in short supply or absent.

I didn't invent this principle.

I was first exposed to it as a sales rep. But during the decades that have followed, I've put it to work everywhere, for my clients and for myself. (How else could I earn five university degrees, teach at forty universities, write a dozen books, compose hundreds of articles, build a nationwide consulting practice, and become an attorney and a martial artist, among other things?)

You've probably applied it without awareness, yet you've also profited by doing so. My contribution is to assert its universality and to show more people how to use it, to advance their careers, their wealth, and their happiness. Its message is optimistic. It says you can do whatever you resolve to do. But unlike most uplifting books (which I also enjoy reading), it doesn't simply promote an idea.

It doesn't seek to change your attitudes or to radically alter your thinking. It strives to change your everyday practices and results. Accordingly, this book isn't about building new skills. It is about putting the skills you have to work on an increasing basis. It doesn't require an aptitude, a knack, or any great insight. Simply put, it is a discipline, a regimen, a more effective deployment of what you know, and a better way of doing what you can do.

You'll see example after example of people in various walks of life who have thrived by putting it to work. We have several names for these people. We think of them as survivors, winners, and sometimes as superhumans. We also think they were born with the right stuff, with whatever that X factor is that makes them incredibly optimistic and resilient.

I have a different explanation. I attribute their wins to their habit of using large -numbers thinking and practices, period.

I believe that it is the only success secret you'll ever need to know!

So please join me in this wonderful adventure as you discover how much more you can achieve and enjoy.

One College Isn't Enough!

I've had innumerable experiences with the Law of Large Numbers, but above all, I'd like to share one with you right away.

A number of years ago, I had finished my PhD at the University of Southern California. I had also accepted a teaching job, and a prestigious one, at a university in the Midwest. The president of the university gave an orientation speech that year as a way of welcoming the faculty, new and old. In that talk, he mentioned that university enrollments were expected to fall for the following fifteen to twenty years because of the low birth rate of Americans.

His message was intended to gird us for adversity, but it had an even more profound effect on me. Frankly, I was shocked that I had hitched my professional wagon to such a falling star. I wasn't going to accept a future, consisting of smaller numbers, sitting down! But I loved teaching and didn't want to leave it. I simply wanted to live prosperously while doing what I loved.

So I asked myself how could I turn small numbers into large ones.

I couldn't personally change the birthrate all that much. But I could increase attendance in my classes if I redirected their focus. So here's what I did.

I decided to teach adults through the continuing-education programs at multiple universities. (There was no shortage of grown-ups.) I calculated that I could earn more money and have more job security, and fun, by teaching short, one-day programs instead of semester-length courses.

Within eighteen months, I was teaching at thirty-five universities from coast to coast. I put together regional and then national tours. In this short time, my income shot up by over 1000 percent.

That, in a nutshell, is the Law of Large Numbers in action. It laid the foundation of a very successful career, and it goes to show that if you do enough of anything, you're bound to succeed and even prosper.

These Little-Town Blues . . .

You've probably heard Frank Sinatra crooning the tune, "New York, New York." It's played over the loudspeakers at Yankee Stadium during ball games. In it he declares, "These little-town blues are melting away . . . "

I like little towns, but unfortunately they don't have large numbers. New York has lots of everything, and it is, as the song says, the "city that never sleeps." That's a big part of its charm—that it's so big!

There are lots of opportunities where there are big numbers. Lots of jobs, potential mates, social diversions, cultural affairs, and yes, even universities. You could invest thousands of lifetimes without exhausting the opportunities and challenges of such a place.

But there are undoubtedly residents of New York and other big cities who use small-numbers thinking, and who never emerge from their shells. What a pity!

Some years Walmart became the top company in the world, measured in sales. It beat out the huge oil company Exxon and the megasoftware firm Microsoft. How did it achieve this mighty task? It sells LOTS of items, and makes LOTS of tiny profits from those individual sales. This is its magical formula: LOTS of really low prices, all the time.

Another company that has made use of the Law of Large Numbers is Super Glue. One of my clients is a company founded by one of the inventors of Super Glue, which you've probably purchased at one time or another. His philosophy is similar.

"Price it by the drop, and sell it by the gallon." This is his winning way to exploit large numbers with a tiny product.

I don't have to tell you about McDonald's, which is the most successful restaurant chain in the world. When Ray Kroc saw the small burger outlet in San Bernardino run by the McDonald brothers, he envisioned more than a tiny company. His vision built a vast, empire that included restaurants at over 37,000 locations by 2018. Like Walmart, McDonald's has a formula of small prices and big sales.

Kroc, by the way, was in his fifties when he hatched the idea of making McDonald's a household name. He probably tried lots of things in his life before the right one came to mind. That's another large-numbers story.

Sales Is a Large-Numbers Game

One of my first and most profound encounters with the Law has been in selling. It is a core truth that you will sell more if you do as one very successful entrepreneur urged his staff, when I was present:

See the people, see the people, and see the people!

As he put it, these are the three Golden Rules of selling.

There's no excuse for doing anything but seeking large numbers, especially if you're in sales or business. The more suspects you have, or people you think might buy, the better off you'll be. These suspects will turn into prospects, and having a lot of them is a happy thing indeed, because lots of prospects will inevitably turn into a good number of sales.

Countless sales managers have admonished their crews that they shouldn't outsmart themselves by settling for smaller numbers of suspects and prospects in their selling pipelines.

There are lots of rationalizations that argue against a large-numbers philosophy. Let's turn to them now, so we can debunk them.

"It's Either Quality or Quantity!"

One stock argument against seeking large numbers in nearly any endeavor is that we are confronted with an inescapable dilemma:

If we seek quantity, we'll necessarily sacrifice quality, and if we go for quality, we'll have to forgo quantity.

Though widely accepted, this is in fact a nonproblem. To better appreciate the operation of quantity and quality, we should examine the widespread problem of writer's block.

Julia Cameron and Mark Bryan have written a book that I'm very fond of: *The Artist's Way*. In it, they help artists of all kinds to get unstuck, and some of their most profound advice is dedicated to writers. Their solution for beating writer's block, which is the inability to get yourself to actually sit down and write anything of value, owes its power to the Law of Large Numbers.

They urge writers to write "morning pages," which consist of three pages of stream-of-consciousness expression, each and every day. These writings are unedited, and they should simply come out any way they wish to come out.

The only purpose of morning pages is to get writers to tap into their unconscious, without judgment. The idea is to simply make yourself do it, and the result will be a freeing of your inhibitions. You'll then feel free to write "serious" stuff, which until that point you had been bottling up.

Morning pages have worked for me! I meandered at first, but soon graduated to writing about 500–1500 words of really decent text each and every day. Many of these items became published articles. Others formed parts of books.

But Cameron and Bryan point out, quite rightly, that if we become obsessed with quality, worrying about whether our stuff will pass muster, we'll never get to square one, and write anything.

By freeing ourselves of the concern about quality, by focusing instead on quantity, quality takes care of itself. Ergo, they have a little artist's prayer: "Great Creator, I will take care of the quantity. You can take care of the quality!"

In other words, quantity often, perhaps inevitably, leads to quality, but it doesn't work the other way around with the same degree of reliability.

Computer Dating

One of the biggest breakthroughs in romance has been ushered in through computer dating. Companies such as Eharmony.com and Match.com have had a huge impact on how people identify potential mates.

These services harness the power of the Law of Large Numbers. You submit your profile to their service and take an inventory consisting of your background, your tastes, and your interests. A profile is then produced that matches you with more suitable candidates than you might meet in a lifetime of personal hit-and-miss searching. You're then able to narrow the list even further to those who you believe might make good partners.

If there has ever been an illustration of how quantity is transformed into quality, computer matchmaking is it. Even if you never use such a service, you can, on a vastly smaller yet still potentially effective scale, do what they do for you.

The key is to identify your interests, isolate those who are most likely to share them, and them "swarm" the ones who fit your profile. For, example, you might accomplish this by joining every arts or Elvis-loving organization you can find if you want to find someone with those interests.

The Man Who Flunked
the Bar Forty-Seven Times

The Law of Large Numbers often masquerades as other virtues. Virtues, you might say, roll up their sleeves and get down to work when they're transmuted into a large-numbers campaign. One of my favorite examples is the persistence shown by Maxcy D. Filer. Mr. Filer attended law school, graduated, and then did what comes next—he sat for the California bar examination.

California's bar exam is known to be one of the most rigorous in the country. Typically, 40–50 percent of first-time takers will fail. Imagine how badly they feel.

They're prevented from practicing law until they pass, and the exam is only offered twice each year. So if you take it and fail, you have to wait a long time before you get another chance to pass it.

Mr. Filer didn't fail the test once, or twice—painful as that may have been. He flunked forty-seven times! Please take a second to process what this means. The exam is given only twice per year. By my calculation, he invested 23.5 years simply to become licensed—and that's after going to law school for three or four years.

Your life, in significant ways, is on hold every time you prepare to take the test and then await your results. Will you be changing jobs? Can you tell a potential employer that you'll become available on a specific date, or will you have to wait, wait, and wait again?

Fortunately, Mr. Filer did pass, and he became a successful practicing lawyer. I was so impressed by his perseverance that I interviewed him by phone. I wanted to discover what kept him going, so I asked him, "What did you tell yourself each time you failed?"

He said, "I didn't think of it as failure. I felt I had passed each time, but it just wasn't recognized yet by the examiners."

Having started his career picking cotton and having held a number of jobs in the interim, he modestly said, "Here I was, sitting next to lawyers who went to Harvard and Yale, and I was simply happy to be there!"

He knew that he would pass sooner or later because he was committed to taking it as many times as it took. That's large-numbers thinking at work.

By the way, because you have to be current in all major areas of the law to succeed on the test, he was probably one of the most updated lawyers in the country by the time he passed.

Virtues and Large Numbers

Several other values are actualized when you put the Law to work. For instance, what is discipline except the habit of doing things a certain way that you've convinced yourself will produce a proper outcome?

Or consider duty, which could be characterized as always doing what you have obligated yourself to do. In that case, you do it a lot because you're doing it all the time!

Honesty is similar. It is the steady practice of telling the truth whether it seems to serve an expedient purpose or not.

Even virtues that seem to pertain to *not* doing can be said to contain a large-numbers component, such as forbearance: you might resist the temptation to scorn or chastise someone, such as a child, because you feel it would be too traumatizing. If the child is a frequent wrongdoer, then you have to flex your forbearance muscles quite a bit. You have to resist doing something that would otherwise seem to come naturally or would at least lend itself to impulsiveness.

Patience is a virtue that works in the same way. It isn't the absence of action, though it may appear to be so. It is the action of waiting, which takes continuing exertion to accomplish. You may be counting the minutes before you feel it is the right time to act.

I think you would be hard put to identify a virtue that doesn't somehow imply, or is not enhanced by, the application of a large-numbers philosophy. Compassion is the steady practice of seeing that you can relate to the circumstances, the thinking, and the faults, as well as to the strengths of all human beings, past or present. It is augmented by counting the ways in which we are similar instead of dissimilar.

Virtues tell us how to become good or better people, and that takes practice! In fact, it's a job that never ends and is therefore one that requires continuous attention. And paying attention, as any young student knows, is always something that requires the steady application of effort.

The Law in Sports

One of my favorite examples of the application of the Law is in sports. For instance, it is well known that home-run king, Babe Ruth, was also the record-holding strike-out king of his era, as was Hank Aaron, the Babe's record-breaking successor, several decades later.

They succeeded AND failed a lot, because they swung at a lot of pitches with a home-run-hitting swing. Implicit in the Law is that if you do enough of anything, you'll fail a lot, but this is the price we pay in order to succeed a lot as well.

Athletes who practice a lot tend to do better than those who don't. They take extra batting practice, field more fly balls and grounders, and generally do more to stay in shape than their less successful peers. But they know something that many other people don't quite realize in the same way. We'll turn to that next.

You Don't Have to Be Perfect!

Fortunately, to be a great hitter, or a great anything else, you don't have to be perfect. Not only that, but the thought that you *can* become perfect or that somehow you *must* become perfect can prevent you from improving.

The reason is that you know, at least unconsciously, that you can't be flawless. No one can be. But if we buy into perfectionism, the idea that it is possible, or mandatory, we'll tend to freeze up, try less, and therefore fail more.

Along this line, it is known that perfectionism leads to procrastination, which is a very bad, small-numbers habit. In fact, procrastination is a shrinking-numbers and then a stopping-numbers habit. It has the same relationship to a large-numbers philosophy that a parked car has to one that is zipping along the Autobahn.

By invoking a large-numbers mentality, you break the back of procrastination by insisting that you take action after action. Procrastination spawns inaction.

Recently I decided to test-market a new seminar. I outlined it and put together a trial brochure, and then I contacted several prospects. At the end of my pilot campaign, I assessed my results.

My first impulse was to simply count the nos that I received in proportion to the yesses. There were a lot more nos, to be sure. But there were a good number of yeses as well, though I was more inclined to emotionally overvalue the negatives.

I contacted forty to fifty people, and I received about 5five positive reactions, one or two of which might lead to significant relationships. Expressed as a raw number, that may not seem too positive. About one in ten liked my concept.

Still, if I had done a direct mailer, conventional wisdom indicates that I would have been lucky to get a 1–2 percent response. So my approach was much more successful than mail, and also faster to execute.

If I replicated this test week after week, and I simply produced the same proportional outcome, I would develop about 100 significant relationships in a year. That's an incredible response, but it takes a large-numbers commitment to bring it about.

Putting perfectionism on hold has its rewards!

Anything Worth Doing Is Worth Doing Poorly

Some successful people change the old aphorism "Anything worth doing is worth doing well," to read "Anything worth doing is worth doing poorly."

Their reasoning is that by trying something, albeit imperfectly and even hastily, or halfheartedly, we have still *started* something, while overcoming the inertia of doing nothing.

A kindred saying, "Well begun is half done," would be modified to read "Begun is half done." In the large-numbers way of seeing things, ATTEMPTS matter a lot. Inevitably, if you do something a long time, or you try something over and again, you're bound to improve.

How can you NOT improve?

Want to play tennis? Swing the racket a lot. Hit the ball a lot. Play a lot of matches.

Looking Good Is Overrated

Of course there will be detractors who will say, "Practice is good, but practicing with the wrong form is detrimental."

They have a point, but here's how I would state it. If you can choose between having good form or bad form, choose better form. But still, practice your enhanced form assiduously.

But here's the sticky part. Most people "choke" when they're required to look good or to emulate professionals, especially when they're first learning something. An emphasis upon correctness tends to dampen one's enthusiasm. Let me give you an example.

I used to enjoy driving a bucket of golf balls every now and then. This very simple activity gave me a lot of satisfaction, because I liked the surge I got when I connected solidly with the ball. After hitting a bucket with my brother-in-law on the famed Pebble Beach course, he remarked that I had potential and lots of power. So he set me up with a golf lesson with the local pro.

I learned the right grip, the right stance, and, I guess, most of the right fundamentals. Oh, and I "unlearned" at least a few "bad" habits.

And I haven't hit a golf ball since.

It just seems too darned complicated! That's not my idea of a good time. I want to jump right into something, and more or less figure it out on my own. Once I feel I'm having fun, I might learn more about the sport, or the craft, or the field.

I know certain family members who won't try anything new unless they take lessons first. Lots and lots of lessons are necessary, they think, before they can solo and try out any activity on their own terms.

But you don't need anyone's approval to try something. Find a point of entry that is useful to you, and have some fun. Sooner or later you'll have to hit the ball or stand up on the surfboard your own way, so what are you waiting for? (By the way, please don't pity me because I haven't played more golf. I understand it's a curse, and I have martial arts, jogging, weight training, and other activities that keep me plenty busy!)

Invest a Day in Numerous Lives

When I graduated from college, I took a job in the leasing business, and one of my clients was an attorney whom I admired quite a lot. Because I planned on going to law school at some point, I asked him if I could hang out with him for a day and simply observe what he did.

He agreed, and we spent a terrific day together. He introduced me to a bunch of people, including the boxer Ken Norton. As we shook hands, my client said, "This is the man who is going to beat Muhammad Ali!" And a few years later, Norton did that, breaking the former champ's jaw in the process.

Anyway, Bob showed me what being a lawyer was about. We spent a lot of time filing documents at courthouses and traveling in and out of the office. I was most impressed with the fact that he was his own boss, and everybody seemed to like and respect him.

I think students and others should spend a career day with people in lots of occupations and professions. This insider's view would save heartaches later on, because aspirants would see what it's really like to work in different fields.

Change Your Definition of *Failure*

Many people avoid doing things in large numbers because they fear failure, and they figure that if they try more, they're bound to experience more of what they fear.

What does it mean when we say we failed?

Thomas Edison was accused of being a failure because he had to conduct thousands of experiments to perfect the light bulb. Reportedly, he bristled that "I didn't fail. I merely discovered thousands of ways in which the bulb didn't work!"

When I consulted for the U.S. Navy at the Naval Research Laboratory in Washington, scientists told me the same thing when we discussed how they measure achievement.

"For us," one of them said, "Failure *is* success." He went on to explain that failing allows scientists to alert their peers to what isn't significant, so they won't waste their time by replicating unfruitful experiments. A long history of failing, in science, is often a precursor of success.

It is a lot like a stonecutter's experience. He may chip away at a rock ninety-nine times without apparent success, but on the hundredth try, suddenly the stone will split in front of him. Was it the "lucky" hundredth blow that did it? It was probably the ninety-nine beforehand that weakened the stone, allowing it to split with the final strike.

It's Usually Too Soon to Throw In the Towel

Most of us would make pretty poor stonecutters, because we'd quit long before attempting a hundred blows. That's because, according to one prominent psychologist, Dr. Albert Ellis, we suffer from low frustration tolerance. LFT, as Ellis abbreviates it, is really the opposite of patience. When we suffer from it, we insist that we must get our rewards NOW! It's like children who constantly ask their parents, "Are we there yet?"

When you foster a large-numbers mentality, you appreciate that it could take quite a while to achieve your goal, but you are prepared to take the time that is required to get the job done. You also know that there is a positive relationship between efforts continued over time and results achieved.

The more frequently you do something, and the longer you do it, the better you will do.

Do You Really Want Washboard Abs?

If there is one exercise that most people seem to hate, it's flexing their abdominal muscles. Even if they're committed to getting into shape, they tend to avoid exercising this area. When exercising, I actually emphasize this area.

What I do is simple. I avoid fats, and I do about 1000 flexions of my abs every day. That's right, 1000!

It takes less time than you think, because a good flex only induces your muscles to move your body a couple of inches at a time. But how did I arrive at 1000 instead of 100 or 750?

I look at it this way. If I do 1000 flexes a day, that's 365,000 per year, and how can my gut do anything but look better, tighten up, and shrink if I am committed to doing this regime? I mean, that's over a third of a million flexes a year! (Actually, I'm shooting for a target of about 1500 flexes a day, so I can get up to a half-million a year.)

Are there days when I don't feel like doing it? You bet! But I know that even if I only do a few hundred repetitions, I'll be way ahead of where I would be if I did nothing.

I realize there will be fitness gurus and fanatics who will say I'm doing too many, or that I should rest a day between workouts, but I don't care. For me, more is better.

Improve Your Social Life

Do you remember what your parents told you after you had broken up with your first girlfriend or boyfriend?

Don't worry. There are lots of fish in the sea.

This was sage advice, though it may not have been a comfort at the time, because we were thinking, "Yeah, but there's only one" Megan or Trevor or whoever.

But their words contain the great secret of developing a happy social life. You simply can't allow your world to devolve into having only one line cast in the stream. You have to have lots of lines constantly trawling for what you want.

A popular radio personality aims his message at single guys. His advice is often pretty brutal, but it all boils down to maintaining large numbers of opportunities. He urges his listeners to have a rotation of people from whom to choose dates.

If one of them becomes the One, well, that's OK. But in the meantime, shuffle the deck, put in pinch hitters, expand your roster, or look at it any way you like. Keep your options open, and when one of your starting pitchers seems to be flaking out or underperforming, say, "Call the bullpen!"

You can't do this until your bullpen is full. So that's job number one. Fill it up.

(It sounds a lot like the formula for getting sales. Lots of suspects lead to lots of prospects, which lead to lots of sales.)

Another way to put it is to keep a lot of irons in the fire, or keep your options open. Not putting all of your eggs in one basket is yet another way of stating the Law.

The Bible Encourages Large-Numbers Thinking

"Be fruitful and multiply" is the Bible's way of encouraging the use of the Law, and we see it in many other significant passages as well.

"Ask and you will receive," implies asking often, and asking a lot of different people who can say yes. To me, "Knock and it shall be opened" must mean more than knocking once on a single door. I interpret it as urging people to find lots of doors and to knock often until doors are answered. The same logic applies to interpreting the verse "Seek, and you will find."

If you lose your keys, you don't search for them only where it's easy to look, like under a lamppost. You need to seek them in every conceivable place in which they may be found. In other words, seek a lot.

Can We Stick with Certain Things Too Long?

I know a successful businessman who is incredibly tenacious. Once he seizes an idea, or, more accurately, once it seizes him, he's committed to it. Nothing will convince him that his new thing doesn't have merit.

He is a poster child for the Law of Large Numbers. When he commits, he continues to draw from his original well of inspiration, come what may. He'll make effort after effort to assure his ventures succeed.

He went into the balloon business during a recent recession. He figured that balloons are probably the cheapest toys that cash-strapped parents can buy for their kids. They're colorful, happy creations. They make people smile, while symbolizing a carefree attitude and celebrations.

His reasoning was sound, but launching the enterprise wasn't easy. He had legal squabbles with a partner, whom he eventually had to buy out. And sales just didn't materialize as he had projected.

I remember thinking, "Why doesn't he jettison this idea and go back to something he knows better, where he has been successful in the past?" Despite my doubts, he "found the key," as he was fond of putting it, and the enterprise became profitable.

What Are the Opportunity Costs?

The businessman's repeated efforts paid off, but could he have done better by refocusing upon some other opportunity? Could he have made more money with fewer hassles and greater enjoyment by pursuing an alternative? In other words, what benefits did he forgo by sticking to balloons? Economists call these unaccessed alternative uses of assets and efforts *opportunity costs*.

Let's say you have accumulated $10,000 that you want to invest. You could buy a small piece of land, or you might use it as a down payment on a vacation property or timeshare. The value of your investment could be projected to rise by, say, 5 percent per year after expenses.

But acquiring the property would mean that you couldn't get 3 percent per year by investing in a tax-free municipal-bond fund, which is virtually risk-free. The fund requires no maintenance, upkeep, or management on your part. You buy it, and then merrily sit on the sidelines.

Real estate, on the other hand, requires more personal initiative and effort. Even with raw land, you need to visit it periodically, or have someone you trust do that for you, so a squatter doesn't accrue any potential rights to it through what is called *adverse possession*.

Could the balloon king have found a more desirable alternative? Would he have been more successful by *not* invoking the Law of Large Numbers?

The Law of Large Numbers Way of Quitting

It might seem as if once you have embraced the Law, you are forced to see EVERYTHING through to a bitter end, even if quitting at an earlier point may have been an easier and more productive course of action. This could happen, but the Law actually encourages you to evaluate alternatives more thoroughly and dispassionately.

Plus you can perform what management guru Peter F. Drucker has termed "systematic abandonment." This practice discourages you from sticking with a loser too long.

Drucker points out that companies often have extensive product lines. There are the original widgets that were created when the firm got under way, which brought in lots of profit and enabled growth to occur. Subsequently, new products have been developed or acquired that have eclipsed the originals in profitability.

But often, says Drucker, senior management is reluctant to phase out the original products. They're emotionally invested in them, and they justify their continuing commitment with sayings like, "WIDGETS built this company!"

The railroads failed to diversify into air travel because they defined themselves as railway firms instead of as more generic transportation companies. Similarly, it took IBM a long time to get out of the mentality that the computers they built had to be large mainframes. They finally started making PCs and laptops, but their hesitation enabled the Dells and others to outperform their reluctant and tardy efforts.

Drucker says that systematic abandonment is the answer to the hardening of attitudes about traditional product lines. He urges companies to continuously identify the items that the market isn't supporting as it should and then to jettison them.

The question to ask is whether, knowing what we do now, we would reenter this market with this product at this time. If the answer isn't a resounding YES, then it is time to get out.

You can see how the Law pertains to even the idea of quitting something. Everything we do should be considered from a large-numbers viewpoint.

The college student who starts with his sights set on obtaining a technical degree in computer science might take a new look at his choice as a sophomore. Figuring that too many of these jobs are being outsourced to India and elsewhere, which is depressing wages here for the positions that remain, he shifts to investment banking as a career goal. By the time he is a senior, he may take yet another look at investment banking and resolve to stay in school to get a graduate degree, to be even more competitive. Revisiting a decision is different from being indecisive. In a rapidly changing marketplace, it is prudent.

Should You Stay in That Relationship?

The person who finds herself in a dead-end relationship with an intimate friend may decide to play the field to improve her chances of finding long-term happiness. She may then have a zillion first dates before she decides upon a suitable new boyfriend. When some lucky person warrants a second date, she may systematically apply her criteria to determine whether to abandon this relationship or keep it going.

Quitting is often perceived as frivolous, immature, and counterproductive. Often we give up too soon. But an equally disturbing tendency is to not give up at all if and when it is warranted. The Law helps you to avoid this tendency by inviting you to be systematic in your abandonment decisions. If you diligently apply the Law to these scenarios, you should feel free of the customary guilt and self-downing that quitting can arouse.

Conquer Your Fears through the Law

Courage has been defined, not as the absence of fear, but as doing what needs to be done despite the fear. Having a certain amount of fear is a normal thing, and in dangerous situations it can be eminently practical, and even life-saving.

But other fears have very little connection to potential death or disability, and we may need to overcome these to enjoy life more and live it more completely.

For instance, you might be afraid of strangers. In a dark alley, this is a good fear to have, but at a company cocktail party it's less appropriate. How do you manage this fear or diminish it so you can have a better time, meet new people, and be a better mixer?

There are two basic ways, each of which invokes the Law of Large Numbers.

One is *systematic desensitization*. I used this one at the beach the other day. Deciding I wanted to interact with more of the people I see every day, I resolved to say hi to at least five people in a two-mile stretch of the jogging path. Most of them were a little surprised that someone broke the silence, but happily so. They grinned or gestured or grunted back belated hellos as we passed by each other.

By making myself say hello to a certain number of folks, I was desensitizing myself to the fear of rejection. If I do this on a deliberate, regular basis—in other words, if I greet people a large number of times day after day—there is bound to be a warming of relations between us.

I'll then be systematically desensitizing myself to my fear of strangers.

This is a classic way to take the power out of our phobias. If you fear elevators, guess what this approach would have you do? That's right—you'd ride them enough to earn frequent-flyer miles.

The key to this technique is that we see that our fears are really unfounded. People don't slug us for saying hello, nor do they overtly reject us. Even if anything negative happened, it would probably be mild, and we could handle it. Plus, the few negative outcomes would be paltry when compared to the wins we created by communicating with lots of new people.

Create an Arithmetic of Success

Salespeople encounter rejection on a regular basis. How do they handle it? Are they simply less sensitive to it than other people?

Salespeople see the Law of Large Numbers as a way to master the arithmetic of success. After they've gained experience, they realize that one in five, or one in twenty-five, people will agree to their proposition. The price they pay to earn that sale is to wade through, or some might say to suffer through, the four or twenty-four others who won't buy.

Some salespeople will mentally break this down into dollars and cents so that the process has a mathematical foundation. Let's say a sale is worth a $100 commission, and it takes twenty-five efforts to result in one. From a mathematical perspective, how much is each effort worth? It's worth $4, right?

Instead of thinking, "Gee, I've made twenty-four presentations and haven't earned a dime," the smart seller tells himself, "No problem. I've earned $96. All I have to do is make one more presentation. I'll be able to earn another $4 and cash in on the entire $100 that have accrued."

In other words, they *expect* to achieve a sale in due time. They do it by using their imagination in a positive way to diminish their fear. This is the second method of using the Law to overcome our fears: *imagine positive outcomes.*

To go back to my jogging example, as I move by each new recipient of my greetings, I will imagine them reciprocating with a friendly hello of their own. By expecting good things, I focus on something positive instead of dreading a bad outcome.

The salesperson looks forward to the smiling face or upbeat email that will endorse his offer and say YES! He makes himself see it in his mind even though the prior twenty-four folks have said no. In other words, he imagines succeeding a large number of times.

By the way, through a positive use of the imagination, the seller enables himself to come across as being confident. And he actually *is* more confident than he would be if he disabled himself by misusing the imagination to anticipate perennial rejections. Knowing that rejection is temporary, he may silently say to his prospect:

"Thank you for rejecting my offer so efficiently! Now I'll have even more time to invest in finding the true sale that I know is dwelling in this list of prospects before me. By the way, I appreciate the $4 that has accrued from my investment of time and effort with you. Bye!"

How to Pursue Scarce Resources

I mentioned that I left a conventional college teaching position to pursue a career in continuing education. But I didn't tell you how challenging it was to earn that original position.

Even though I had all of the required degrees, including my doctorate from a fine university, as well as four prior years of teaching experience, it wasn't a foregone conclusion that I would get hired. A temporary incumbent held the job. This person was well liked and wanted to be hired permanently. Candidates from across the country were also interested in it. You might say it was the trophy job of the season in an otherwise dismal hiring market.

How did I use the Law of Large Numbers to get a one-of-a-kind reward? Typically, three letters of recommendation are required when you apply. I had at least five or six sent. I not only made the initial application, but I also frequently checked in with the school to track my progress. Instead of being satisfied with visiting the campus once, I welcomed the opportunity to go there twice. I also had a number of influential people call the hiring authorities.

I STILL DIDN'T GET THE JOB!

The temp got it, and if you think about it for a minute, that makes sense. He was there, he had strong student evaluations, and he got along with his peers. In fact the position description may have been written with him in mind.

Everyone I knew was amazed that I had been passed over. Nonetheless, this didn't stop me. I wrote thank-you letters to the influential people at the college, mentioning my continuing interest in the job if circumstances changed. The chairman of my department, who was also my advisor, stayed in touch with them.

Finally the heavens parted. The temp accepted a new position that had opened up at a school a few hundred miles away. I got what I wanted!

At first I lost, but through my unrelenting large-numbers campaign, I prevailed at last.

This reminds me of the famous remark by Yogi Berra, "It ain't over until it's over!"

Remember this: it isn't over until YOU say it is, until you make that decision. Generally, if you're willing to take nearly anything to the human limit, you'll finally win.

I forget who said it, but the statement still applies: no problem can withstand a constant assault of effort on your part. If you're committed to finding the answer, or inventing one, or generating a substitute, you can do it.

Never Tell Me the Odds!

If you're a science-fiction fan, you've undoubtedly seen the Star Wars movies. In the original, Han Solo is captaining his escape vessel when one of his cohorts asks him if he realizes how low his chances are of succeeding.

He snaps back, "Never tell me the odds!"

I've always loved that line because it says, "The odds don't apply to me. I'll be the exception to the rule." As Stonewall Jackson remarked, one courageous person makes a majority.

Make your own odds. When you do more of nearly anything, you've improved your chances of winning. Even the lottery becomes more winnable if you purchase more tickets!

Get In and Spread Out

At Xerox, I met a sales manager who had a really good marketing idea. Once you have penetrated an account, say by meeting and befriending a vice-president of operations, it's time to meet other potential clients within the broader client organization. Call on the vice president of sales and marketing, or try to set a meeting with the president.

The manager called this his "get in and spread out" philosophy, and it has worked for me on numerous occasions. It validates the Yogi Berraism about something not being over until it's over. It also gives weight to the idea that by spreading out you can shift the odds of succeeding in your favor.

Recently I inaugurated a marketing campaign aimed at lawyers. I phoned into a number of firms providing continuing education to see if they were interested in sponsoring a new seminar that I was testing.

The first call I made was to a major association of lawyers—about 500 strong, across California. The contact's name was on the Internet, and so I smiled-and-dialed, as they say.

A woman answered the phone with a suspicious "hello," which didn't seem very welcoming. I mentioned my seminar and my interest in having her association run it. She seemed frustratingly elusive as to whether she saw merit in the idea. She said she'd run it by the board of directors, but they didn't meet for two months.

As you can imagine, I wasn't thrilled on a few counts. First, I figured that she was going to be a really reluctant champion of my idea, and if she did bring it up, it would be in an atmosphere of negativity. Moreover, I didn't like the idea of waiting.

After I hung up with her, I returned to the website from which I got her name. After a click or two, I saw a comprehensive listing of her board of directors and other powerful persons in the association. Their titles, phone numbers, and even email addresses were there.

I GOT IN AND SPREAD OUT! I wrote an email indicating that I spoke to her, and then I got into my offer. (I didn't misrepresent the character of our conversation by saying she suggested that I contact them; nor did I say she valued my intentions.) Then I pasted in the description of my program.

Within a few hours, I had phoned and emailed about eighteen people. A few of the people responded favorably, and one asked me for a fee schedule. But after I replied, the lawyer who inquired about fees said no, seemingly on behalf of the entire association.

I didn't reply to this rejection. I wanted to see if anyone would overrule him, or have a different reply. A few days later, I got my answer from the president. He said he discussed the proposal, and the right person from my region, southern California, would be communicating with me about speaking opportunities.

It wasn't over when I made my first call, and it wasn't over when that other person seemingly took it upon himself to reject my offer. It still isn't over. My offer LIVES!

Of course, I'm beaming as I write these words. The Law of Large Numbers says that getting in and spreading out is the best way to optimize your odds of achieving positive results. If you allow any one person to speak for a complex entity, you're doing yourself a major disservice.

I've validated this practice before with direct mail. Instead of mailing a single brochure to a company, I would mail five or six to various functionaries. What would happen is really exciting. They would converge on the person most likely to be the champion of the seminar, and that person, with several of my brochures in hand, would contact me.

Large Numbers Will Turn You into a Force of Nature

College-football coach John Robinson said that winning and losing are significant but not all that important in collegiate athletics. What really counts "is who you become in the process" of winning and losing.

He's right, and the same can be said of invoking the Law. By using this precept, by putting it into practice, you transform yourself into someone much more potent and effective, and of course more successful, than the ordinary person.

The great majority of people may want to achieve success just as much as you do, but they don't quite understand how to pay the price, how to get down into the trenches of making their dreams come true. As you work with the Law, you'll notice that a transformation takes place. You will pay the price, and you'll earn the rewards of doing so. After seeing concrete results, you'll experience a surge of motivation to continue. That's when this process becomes fun.

But danger lurks ahead, because you can become a victim of your own success if you're unwary.

Keep Doing What Made You Successful

When you achieve with the Law, you'll be tempted to cut back in your efforts. It's one of the quirks and risks of success.

A few years ago, I worked my way out of a slump by invoking the Law. I made scores of new contacts and offered my articles to websites and to publications. I proposed relationship after relationship and accepted nearly each and every opportunity that came along.

This was like digging my way out of a muddy rut. Before too long, I got through the mushy stuff and reached solid ground. Soon I was busy with well-paying work.

But then, because I was in the habit of marketing, I started receiving more offers than I could personally handle. Instead of referring these out, which would have been smart, I cued them up and tried to service them myself.

I got so superbusy that I could hardly breathe. The money was rolling in, but I was steadily burning out. Finally I had to shut everything down simply to rest and recuperate. When I tried to ramp up my sales again, I sputtered and spun my wheels. How come?

I had conveniently forgotten the kind of large-numbers campaign that I had undertaken to get so busy in the first place. Until I realized that I needed to cover all of the bases again, I didn't make any headway. Only by committing once more to work the numbers assiduously did I navigate my way out of the slump.

Ideally, we should get busy with productive work. But we should also remember to simultaneously plant new seeds for future business, and if we can, we should endeavor to find better ways to grow our capacity to sustain our achievement routines at full bore.

Small-Numbers Voodoo and How to Avoid It

I've been extolling the beauty of large numbers, and I suspect that people intuit this great principle to be a sound one. They know it works, but they only put it to use on a hit-and-miss basis.

Why?

There are competing doctrines and viewpoints that confuse people into discounting the efficacy of the large-numbers approach. I'm going to discuss them here.

Always a Bride, Never a Bridesmaid

It may be OK to marry a person, providing we're confident they are the One, and they constitute the best choice available. Sadly, most folks can't be confident that they've made the best decision because they really haven't exercised CHOICE.

Choosing implies that we are selecting from alternatives. Many people only allow themselves to get serious with one person, whom they then marry. That doesn't give them a database of experience in interpersonal intimacy. If they perceive a choice, it is between loneliness and having someone's company, and typically a majority of us will elect the latter.

Our romantic literature celebrates a small-numbers mentality when choosing a lifetime mate. It is considered not only proper but sweet if we marry the girl or boy next door, or our high-school sweetheart.

Certainly some of these unions work out, but many don't. Citing their lack of maturity and experience, those who divorce are convinced that they would have acted differently if they had known more people before settling down with one.

People who don't seem to have a prime candidate for marriage are made to feel flawed. "What's wrong with you?" others inquire. They don't generally accept singles who say they are waiting for the right person to come along. Accused of being "too picky" and "unable to commit," people who resist marrying early, or bonding with one of the first people to come along, can find themselves in a constant state of having to explain themselves.

All they're doing is applying LARGE-NUMBERS WISDOM! Power to them!

We Also Marry Our Schools, Jobs, and Stockbrokers

Small-numbers voodoo afflicts us outside of the marital context as well. Too frequently, we settle for just one institution or functionary to serve our needs.

Countless investors stick with losing stockbrokers out of sympathy, superstition, or simple inertia. I kept one fellow on my payroll, so to speak, for many years, and I had never made a dime with him.

If I invested money professionally, on behalf of a large entity, such as a pension fund, I'd have to perform due diligence, and my investment choices would be subject to periodic review. I'd have to justify standing by while an advisor continued to leach assets.

I couldn't get away with saying, "Oh, I like him," or "I've been doing business with him for ten years!" I'd hear a reply such as, "So what?" or "Too bad!" or "Tough for him!"

The established investment community encourages blindly following investment advisors and sticking to bad decisions. They call it a buy-and-hold philosophy. Citing long-range statistics, they assert that over time, the market will rise by about 9–10 percent per year, so never sell your stocks. That's just small-numbers voodoo!

Why Get All Your Degrees
from the Same Place?

The same thinking applies to choosing colleges or graduate schools. Lots of people elect to get their master's degrees at the same place where they got their bachelor's. Why? They know where to park and where to eat, and they also know some of the faculty.

It's easier to just keep going where you've gone before. But for most people this is not a good idea. I did my BA and MA at the same place, which then hired me to teach, and supported me through a PhD program at another school. So I'm an exception, and I'm grateful.

But as a general rule, it is healthy to learn from as many people as possible, because you are receiving their wisdom, which comes from a still wider range of people and institutions. In academic terms, spreading out to new institutions militates against inbreeding, which can be intellectually stunting and corrupting.

The Womb-to-Tomb Illusion

Do you know anybody who is looking for the perfect job or the best employer in the world? It's sad, but lots of folks are wasting their time doing just this. They think there is a job that is so interesting, so lucrative, and so permanent that they can simply hire on and never have to make another employment decision in their lives.

If you haven't been keeping up with the downsizing and outsourcing of America, I'm here to tell you that it doesn't work like this anymore, even if it once did. Here's what's likely to occur to you even if you think you're currently experiencing occupational bliss.

Valerie was an ideal employee at an airline. She worked in the systems-analysis unit, and she was so pleased with what she was doing that she shaped her bachelor's degree program after it. She was pursuing her BS degree at night at a local university.

Her company, which had been in business since the end of World War II, sold out to an upstart airline that happened to be more profitable. Her job was moved from California to the East Coast.

She faced a choice: give up her local friends and hangouts, or kiss her job goodbye.

She decided not to make the move, and she has never found a company or a situation where she had felt so respected and valued as she had felt before the buyout.

Of course, the firm that devoured her unit wasn't all that benevolent either. Within record time, it asked its workers to suffer through round after round of wage and benefit cuts.

You've heard that the only constant is change, haven't you? Well, companies have an odd way of acknowledging this fact. They promote the appearance of stability, because it encourages the best workers to hang around and to perform with relative peace of mind.

But like the earth itself, companies are floating on tectonic plates. When they shift, whether from competitive or overall economic pressures, an earthquake is unleashed upon those who aren't true stakeholders.

If you're a realist, you'll play the same game that your employer is playing. They always look for cheaper labor, machines, and computers to automate processes, and they're willing to ditch their people without hesitation when it makes economic sense.

Always job-hunt, if you rely upon being employed by others. Take something better the instant it appears, and never, ever look back. Leverage today's job by seeking tomorrow's.

Use the Law of Large Numbers. If you don't have the time to personally conduct a perennial job hunt, hire one or more headhunters to do it for you. Never, ever stop.

Because if you do, even to smell the roses in the reception area, that could be the time that you'll have the rug pulled out from under you. It will be quite inconvenient, and very hard, to get your next position under just-fired circumstances.

Never Give Away Exclusive Rights

Everybody seeks to be your one and only, but don't let this happen. Let me give you a personal example.

I was thinking of buying a vacation property in Florida on a very small island off the Gulf Coast. Before looking into it, I asked a client, a multimillionaire who seemed plugged into the entire Florida economy, how he would proceed if this were his goal.

"First of all," he said, "I'd be ready to move fast if something came on the market at an attractive price. But the key is to be the first to know when something becomes available. Get yourself three or four realtors to look for investments for you. One of them is bound to find something good before too long."

I remember wondering whether three or four realtors *would* work for me at the same time. This seems naive now, but I actually thought that ethically I had to settle for one person representing me at a time!

Do you see how small-numbers voodoo creeps into one's consciousness? It's true that every realtor wants sole representation, but there is no law that says you have to agree to give anyone an exclusive, no matter how "normal" or "customary" they say it is.

Laziness May Be Your Greatest Foe

It's one matter to deal with other people who want to impose their small-numbers voodoo on us. But it's even harder to cut through our own self-delusions. It just seems to be part of human nature to want to take the easy way out and to resist changing anything if it isn't broken.

If we succumb to these tendencies, we're only being lazy. It's not criminal, to be sure, but it isn't smart either.

Our overall happiness and well-being at any time will be tied to our range of choices. The more choices we have, generally speaking, the freer and more at ease we'll feel.

The Law of Large Numbers is an operational philosophy that encourages you to constantly invent choices. Almost every frustration you'll encounter can be analyzed from a small- versus large-numbers perspective.

Are you in a dead-end job? What makes it such an uncomfortable place to be?

It's only uncomfortable if we feel that we're stuck, that we haven't any alternatives. The second something else opens up, or even if we feel things could be worse, we are informed by larger numbers of possibilities, and we perk up.

Let a Thousand Flowers Bloom

Someone once remarked that nature loves diversity. Otherwise why would there be so many kinds of plants, flowers, and creatures of all kinds?

Why would human beings be athletic and intellectual, and so capable of greatness in so many ways?

Variety is the antidote to dullness. It is an ongoing invitation to excitement and surprise. And it is our birthright by inhabiting this planet at our time in human history. So why wouldn't we want to let a thousand flowers bloom?

The Psychology of Flow

One of our basic urges and satisfactions lies in creativity. We love to make things, shape and reshape them, and make the unseen—that which appears in our hearts and minds—seen.

You've heard people say how their moments of creativity have been joyful and completely involving. Painters merge with their canvases, sculptors with their clay, and writers report that poems, articles, and books seem open new worlds for them.

At times of peak performance, we experience a forgetting of the self, a transcendence of ego and temporal concerns and a merging with our activity that one psychologist calls *flow*. In his book *Flow*, Dr. Mihaly Csikszentmihalyi maintains that we feel most alive, most human, when we have found the secret of losing ourselves in our work or play. This is when we have optimal experiences.

Some people, especially athletes, call it being *in the zone*. When you're in the zone, you can do no wrong. Every stroke of the racket, every swing of the bat feels just right. It's an ideal feeling, and I'm happy to say I've experienced it as a teacher, a public speaker, a salesperson, a lawyer, an athlete, and a writer.

George Gilder, writing about quantum mechanics in his book *Microcosm*, says that when we examine the subatomic universe, we see that friction decreases to such a point that actions seem effortless. That's what being in the zone feels like. There is no reason to strain, and there's no hurry. Everything will turn out well—we're convinced of it. All we have to do is go along with the action.

One of the best pathways into the zone is the Law of Large Numbers.

For instance, when you as a salesperson know there are plenty of prospects that are simply waiting for the chance to buy, you can relax. The strain leaves the selling equation. There's only strain when a scarcity mentality takes over—when we feel there are too few people to contact, that our capabilities are limited.

As a ballplayer, if you know you're going to get another three or four at-bats during a game, you don't have to replay and do penance for your strikeout from your first. If after we break up with someone, another very attractive individual smiles at us and greets us warmly, it sends a signal that we're desirable. Whether or not that gesture leads to something, we take a win from the encounter.

Party planners and realtors will both tell you that one of the best things a get-together can have going for it is a positive flow from room to room. People can circulate, getting chances to chat with lots of others. Inevitably, where there is flow, people have a good time.

List Your Victories

Ours is an abundant universe, and it's only a delusion that encourages us to impose scarcity thinking on it. Whenever you feel down, what's one of the best things you can do?

Make a list of your past victories. Start from birth—hey, you got here! Do you realize how many of your ancestors it took to simply get you to this marvelous stage? It took multiple generations of winners simply to survive to sire you, so that makes you a winner as well. You come from hardy stock indeed!

Your personal assets are abundant. Count them. Count your blessings, as they say. You'll be impressed.

If you're feeling depressed, you've probably convinced yourself somehow that today will look as bleak as yesterday, or that you're descending on a downward slope. Hard as it may be, pull out a piece of paper and list the things that you have going for you that others would envy or admire.

There Is No Such Thing as a Money Problem

Are you running low on cash? Are the bills piling up? Do you feel that you'll never be able to earn a better living?

Countless people have felt the same way, but some of them have turned things around. How did they do it?

One way or another, they put large numbers to work.

I'm very fond of the author Dr. Robert Schuller. His books are incredibly uplifting, and often he has a fresh take on things that is very much worth considering.

Schuller says there is no such thing as a money problem. He says, "It's an IDEA problem."

Think about it for a minute, and I'm sure you'll agree that his statement is profound. Is there a shortage of money in the universe? I mean, is there absolutely *no* money that you can rightfully earn if you put your mind and your effort into it? Is there a czar of money who has proclaimed that you cannot earn a better share, no matter what you do?

If you're saying, "That's right, buddy, there's none for me," you're trapping yourself into scarcity thinking. There are unlimited ways of earning money honestly and responsibly, providing you're ready to devise a large list of ideas.

Thinking Big Requires Large-Numbers Thinking

A few years ago I consulted for a very successful software company. One day, at lunchtime, I ran into the CEO and founder of the firm, and I asked her if she wanted to share a table.

We chatted about how my project was progressing, and then we delved into an even more exciting topic: her ascent to the top.

Her software company had gone public the prior year, and her personal stock holdings were worth several million dollars at the time. I wanted to know what kind of person could conceive of such a successful enterprise. I asked her, "Did you always anticipate that your company would grow as big as it has?"

"Sure," she confidently replied. "I always planned for it to be big. I wouldn't have bothered with it otherwise."

I admire her viewpoint. So many people settle for mediocre results that it's pathetic. The true winners in life always have at least one eye peeled for the prospect of having a breakout success at some point.

People Love to Participate in Something Big

Robert Schuller agrees that it's sometimes easier and more satisfying for everyone to participate in a grand design, one that involves large numbers.

He succeeded in building his internationally famous Crystal Cathedral because he appreciated the value of thinking and acting big. He realized that if he sought to raise funds for a spectacular project—one that would truly be a living monument to his faith and to that of his congregants—he would be more successful than if he sought to construct something more modest.

His insight was that people love to be part of something big because it makes them feel big in the process. Don't you feel the same way?

Make your own projects big and inspiring, and you'll be motivated to achieve more. If you shoot for the stars, you may reach the moon, and that's a lot farther out than where you started.

Watch Great Runnings Backs Run

You might be thinking that it sounds good to always be thinking in terms of achieving large numbers, but sometimes it just isn't realistic. There will be times when you're simply prevented from achieving as much as you'd like.

Granted, we can't win them all, but we can always go for the gusto. I find inspiration in the way great running backs go about doing their jobs in football. Depending upon their team's field position, there are several things they can achieve.

They can get a few inches, a few feet, or a few yards, and earn a first down. This will give their team four new plays that they can execute. Or they can break free, rack up big yardage, and score a touchdown.

Guess what they always have in mind.

Even if they can get a first down with ease, they always want to break loose. Their real goal is to score, and to help their team to score in large numbers so they can win championships. Just like the software entrepreneur, they always have thinking big as part of their game plan, from beginning to end.

Interval Training:
A Great Way to Rack Up the Numbers

If you've used an exercise cycle at any well-appointed gym, you know that most of them have enough gadgetry to keep you amused while you get a good workout. Some stairclimbers offer various programs that will automatically vary the intensity of your activity, making it more interesting and rewarding.

This is a smart concept, and we should do the same thing with our large-numbers campaigns. I mentioned that I do hundreds of abdominal exercises each day. But to break the monotony, I'll change how many I do at a given sitting. Some days I find it pleasurable to go for a hundred straight. Today I did sets of fifty. It all added up to the same figure in the end, but I found today's pace relatively leisurely. Heck, it was Saturday! Why not?

A large-numbers campaign shouldn't burn you out, but it can do just that if you aren't mindful about pushing yourself too far or too long with any specific activity. I strongly believe that by introducing variety, you'll be adding to your overall motivation and you'll be more likely to stick to your campaign until you reach or exceed your goals.

The great behavioral psychologist B.F. Skinner seems to agree with me on this point.

The Schedule of Rewards Can Be More Important than Their Amount

Have you ever wondered why people become compulsive gamblers? I don't know all of the reasons, but B.F. Skinner points out that humans are creatures of reinforcement. Generally, we seek positive rewards while avoiding negative ones. When it comes to money, more is usually better as far as we're concerned, and we generally prefer to win it than to lose it. Most gamblers know that the odds favor the house, and that if they keep playing most games of chance long enough, they'll lose. But they still lose anyway. How come? After all, losing is more painful than winning, and therefore we should shun it and prefer to preserve our dwindling resources.

Skinner says that isn't how motivation works. He says that the schedule of rewards, how often we win, is more significant in getting us hooked on a game than the amount of money we make, or, for that matter, the amount we lose.

A staggered reinforcement schedule hooks us more than a steady one, Skinner says. Winning one out of every three hands of blackjack will potentially give us a greater surge of satisfaction than winning every time. If we won every time, theoretically we'd get rich, but we'd also bore ourselves nearly to death.

Therefore be aware of your own motivational schedule, and then maximize it.

Commissions Aren't for Everyone

I've been a salesperson most of my life, if you add up the time I've spent working both for corporations and for myself. And I can tell you this about my motivation: I prefer to be compensated on a straight commission schedule. This pay plan rewards you when you sell, but when you don't sell, you earn nothing. It sounds harsh, doesn't it? But I like it, because as a rule, when you're a straight commission seller, you earn more money, because companies pay large commissions in this kind of situation. They are likely to feel that they're rewarding you for bringing in business, and for nothing else.

As an entrepreneur, you're in a similar situation. You can keep every dime you earn over and above your expenses and taxes. There are no limits.

Now here's what's interesting. If you average my earnings across the last twenty years when I've been paid this way, and then you compare my average to the salaries and benefits of ordinary professionals, who have been paid more of a flat fee for services, we come out at about the same place.

But I *feel* I've made more money, and objectively I have, if you look at what I've been able to achieve when I've had exceptional years. In those cases, I've invested my surpluses and have derived income from those investments. Had I been salaried, I wouldn't have accumulated enough money in a short enough period to do the same thing.

So there have been ancillary benefits. But you pay an emotional price, because you're riding an income roller-coaster. It's a common tendency to get down on yourself when things aren't going well and to be overly self-congratulatory when they are.

Anyway, setting up your rewards so they comport with your psyche is important, and I encourage you to consider how you like to be paid. Remember, as Skinner points out, the schedule of rewards is often more important that the amount.

Don't Take Your Cues from Others

One of my favorite authors is psychologist Wayne Dyer. I feel that I have grown up with him since reading his first book, *Pulling Your Own Strings*.

By no means was it a foregone conclusion that this book was destined to become a best-seller. In fact, Dyer engaged in his own large-numbers campaign to make it happen.

From his own account, he quit his college teaching post (a man after my own heart) and loaded his old station wagon with thousands of copies of his book, which he had bought at wholesale. Then he toured the country, getting on every radio station that would have him, and speaking at every bookstore he could. Finally, after months and months of relentless exertion, he personally transformed an obscure book into one that was featured on NBC's *Tonight Show*.

During this time, Dyer had plenty of detractors who did not believe that one author could make such a mark in the publishing world by executing a grass-roots campaign. But he believed in himself and in the significance of his message, and he made his dream of success come true. His thoughts have affected millions of people. But he marched to his own drummer, which means he had to turn a deaf ear to those who felt he was on a hopeless journey and utilizing a low-probability rewards plan. He saw the large number of readers he could reach, and he also saw the large number of efforts that he'd have to make in order to reach them.

Should I Have Started with Mahogany?

When I was going to college, I was watching my pennies, which isn't all that unusual. I made a point of using whatever I could find in thrift shops and elsewhere. If there was an abandoned piece of furniture awaiting the garbage truck, I'd snatch it from the curb, if I had a use for it. One day I saw a stack of empty orange crates in the trash outside of a corner grocery store.

I took one home, thinking it would make a nice end table for my girlfriend. I went to the hardware store and bought a couple of grades of sandpaper, for less than a buck, as I recall. Then, in my spare hours, days, and months, I transformed the splintery crate into a very smooth product. I stained it and sealed it, and presented it to my girlfriend as a present. She seemed grateful and genuinely pleased with it, and that made me happy.

Some years later, I made the mistake of mentioning this crate to a different girlfriend. She quipped, "Imagine what you could have made if you had started with mahogany!"

It was a clever remark, I thought. Indeed, what could I have made with the same effort? But here's how I look at her remark today.

She was saying that, compared to my former girl-friend, *she* was mahogany.

OK, that's her opinion, and she's entitled to it. But she missed the fact that I didn't have enough money to buy mahogany. Plus, it was a labor of love. To me, the large numbers of efforts that I had to make with the sandpaper were more than justified.

Here's my point: Only you can determine what's a suitable task in which to invest substantial efforts. Resist taking your cues from other people, no matter how near and dear they may seem to you. In the long run, you may find that you're the only one who sees the beauty in a cast-off piece of wood, but no matter. You are the only person you need to please. Remember this.

Lose Often Enough and You'll Finally Win!

A few years ago, the Detroit Tigers nearly lost more games than any team in baseball history. I think they dodged earning that distinction by a single game. Ironically, the Tigers probably received more publicity outside of the Detroit market than they had since they last won a pennant, many, many moons before. And I'm sure that there were at least some new fans that were starting to cheer for the hapless club, much like the cults that follow the New York Mets, the Chicago Cubs, and the Boston Red Sox.

It's ironic, but you can be so bad that in a way you become good. You occupy a class, in itself. You're a record breaker, but in reverse.

How do you become such a wrong-way legend? In all likelihood, it is a large-numbers achievement.

If you think about it, laurels seem to go to big winners and to big losers, but not to those who find themselves in the indistinguishable middle of the pack. I suppose they are the great majority who don't do enough of anything to be noticed!

What Price Will You Pay?

You can accomplish nearly anything if you're willing to pay the price.

Earlier I spoke of Maxcy Filer, who wanted so much to be a lawyer that he was willing to pay the price of experiencing twenty-three and a half years of testing setbacks to become one.

But I didn't mention that Mr. Filer was probably willing to pay an even higher price. If it had taken that gentleman the remainder of his life, I'm convinced, having spoken to him, that he would have paid that price.

Abraham Lincoln lost almost every campaign for elective office that he entered until he became president of the United States. Obviously he wanted to perform public service, and he was able to shrug off what, to a lesser person, would have been a string of humiliating failures and move forward despite them.

Most obstacles aren't insurmountable, as Robert Schuller points out. He says when we're facing a mountain of resistance, we can choose from several alternatives. We can climb over it. We can try to go around it. We can dig under it. We can tunnel through it. If all else fails, we can figure out a way to make the most of it as it looms before us.

In other words, we almost always have choices that we can make, tactics that we can try.

Make a Decision

Usually, when I've felt the weakest emotionally, I've been stuck in a quagmire of indecision. Not being convinced of the right path to take, I've spun my wheels, or I've taken half-hearted steps toward various goals and then retreated, simply to take timid steps toward others.

Committing to something—to nearly anything, for that matter—makes your life so much easier. You're willing to perform the large number of efforts that it might take to accomplish your task.

Martial Artists Know about Commitment

Yesterday was Easter Sunday. Earlier in the week, one of my martial-arts instructors mentioned that he was going to come into the dojo for the regularly scheduled three o'clock class. As it turned out, three of us made it in, and we had a good class.

Afterwards my instructor mentioned that when he was in his teens, he had passed by the dojo with his friends, and something clicked for him.

"I'm going to become a black belt," he told himself. He made it come true.

Since its founding in 1972, our dojo has only elevated twenty people to the rank of black belt. (I was the twentieth.) It takes eight to ten years or more to earn that distinction, and you need to overcome many difficulties in its pursuit.

In the martial arts, you absolutely have to commit to a large-numbers program. Your body needs to get used to doing certain things effectively, with the correct form, whenever you tell it to. Moreover, you need to train it so it acts unconsciously, doing the best moves, seemingly on its own, in emergency situations.

To become good, you need to perform and practice every strike, kick, block, fighting stance, and sequence of moves countless thousands of times over the years.

This seems like a very big price to pay, and in many ways it is. But you build on this large-numbers commitment. You develop a strength of character that is very different than that of the average person.

The Large-Numbers Secret to Growing Rich

A few years ago, I came across a fascinating book by psychologist Srully Blotnick. *Getting Rich Your Own Way* chronicles the occupational journeys of hundreds of people that Blotnick studied over the course of more than twenty years. Some garnered enough wealth to be classified as bona fide millionaires. Others performed in a more average range economically. Blotnick found that millionaires didn't necessarily make it their goal to achieve wealth. They didn't gravitate toward certain professions or occupations while shunning others.

What distinguished them was the fact that they mastered something. They may have labored in relative obscurity in their fields for years. But by sticking with a pursuit, they came to understand it better than their peers, and their heightened abilities were sought out more and more. Finally, they found themselves in a class by themselves with respect to income, which they invested in various ways.

They grew rich almost unawares!

Blotnick mentions that most of these folks were fascinated with their endeavors, so much that they gladly invested the time it took to become true experts. They made consistent, large-numbers efforts, geared to a singular area. This made them very special achievers in the long run.

By the way, those with more formal education only earned more money in their first few years in the labor market. Over the long term, the differences in earnings between the more and less educated groups diminished significantly.

Blotnick's research tells us that there is no ONE path to wealth. Any path will take you there, providing you get to know it well, and you exercise continuing efforts to master it.

The Large-Numbers View of Life

One of the most respected film directors of the twentieth century was John Cassavetes. His movies had a quirky realism to them that has been emulated by many filmmakers, and it can be seen in some of today's most interesting features.

Cassavetes was famous for allowing his actors to improvise their dialogue. He was fascinated by what would be said long after conventional directors would cry out, "Cut!"

Dinner scenes would seem to go on forever, but there was wisdom in this. Cassavetes knew that the really interesting stuff in family meals came out long after the meal was consumed. Only when people were relaxed and their physical appetites sated would they reveal what their other unfulfilled appetites were.

You wouldn't see these motivations, or even have a remote awareness of them, unless you hung around long enough in the dining room to really come to know the characters.

By encouraging scenes to roll on and on, Cassavetes introduced a large-numbers sensibility into small films, and the result was stunning. Try this in your own life. Let conversations continue just a little longer than you think is normal, and listen to what comes out.

It may be the best part of the encounter.

Make Monotony Your Friend

Sometimes people feel an aversion to a large-numbers philosophy because it t seems boring or monotonous to implement.

I think it can be, and possibly MUST be, monotonous, but not necessarily boring. Here's the difference.

A Zen master can meditate all day while staring at a brick wall. The wall never changes, so it is a monotonous activity. But the master's mind is constantly changing, so he isn't bored by any means.

The challenge is to quiet the mind so that a higher level of consciousness can be reached. Constant distractions are diverting and create a sense of novelty, but they teach us very little about ourselves.

Gandhi found the monotony of nature very appealing. He praised the monotony of necessary human occupations for their service to us all. He was also quick to point out that the monotonous cycles of nature, such as the rising and setting of the sun, are beautiful and comforting.

Grooves Aren't Ruts

Most businesspeople consciously strive to create rational routines. They're rituals that produce consistent results.

A restaurant chef dons his apron and starts and cleans his grill. His vegetable bins are filled. Waiters makes sure that sufficient place settings are on each table. As these tasks are being done, the respective functionaries are also gearing themselves to serving a certain number of people during that shift. The sum total of these routines gets them into a groove.

Working well with other people entails a smooth calibration of these routines. The longer people work with each other, the more they can collaborate seamlessly, making the customer feel that everything is being done effortlessly.

Develop Performative Discipline

A long-running Broadway show is a masterful blending of skills and responsibilities. When people are in the groove, and each is playing her part, the show can go on to be a hit. But there must be consistency from one performance to the next. Keeping a show's energy and balance intact requires discipline, especially when there is a turnover among the show's leading players.

This takes a large-numbers philosophy and commitment.

When I was in high school, I had the privilege of being directed in plays by John Ingle, who went on to star in a daytime soap opera and has had a long and distinguished career in the theater. He taught me the importance of having a "show must go on" sense of urgency and purpose. He called it *performative discipline*, and it has served me well. Each performance, he said, must be your best, and you're simply not permitted to relax or to lose your edge until the show is over.

I had to run seminars on a number of occasions when my voice was succumbing to laryngitis. Instead of having dinner with associates between sessions, I'd rest my voice so I would have enough gas in the tank for the coming session. If I hadn't disciplined myself, I would have failed to reach the high standard Mr. Ingle had insisted we sustain.

Showing up to work at any job on time and ready to produce takes performative discipline. It is yet another important face of the Law of Large Numbers.

Winning Is a Habit

Most of us have heard the famous pronouncement of coaching legend Vince Lombardi: "Winning isn't everything; it's the only thing!" Most people don't know that he also said, "Winning isn't a sometimes thing—it's an all-the-time thing." It's a habit, he said, and so, unfortunately, is losing.

I really like the second quote, because it implies the price we have to be willing to pay to become champions. We have to seek victory on a consistent basis, and we can't allow ourselves to settle for second best.

It takes large numbers of victories to be champions. Everybody loves the feeling of an occasional win, but how many of us set our sights on achieving this outcome time after time, effort after effort?

It's Smarter to Work Harder

You've probably heard people urging each other to work smarter, not harder. Salespeople embrace this saying because they're always trying to improve their productivity, and if they can find a smarter way of closing deals, they'll jump on it.

Unfortunately, this aphorism, like many others, is flawed. If we could choose an easier way to do something, well, why not do it? It's easier to use a washing machine than to beat your clothes clean by the riverside, isn't it? So what is to be gained by turning back the clock and performing a task in a prehistoric way? Unless it is for the purpose of historical reenactment—so you can feel what our ancestors felt—it doesn't seem to be worthwhile. Progress is generally a good thing.

But the apparent choice between working hard and working smart is spurious. In many endeavors, working hard *is* working smarter, while trying to avoid hard work is stupid.

Let's go back to selling for a minute. Let's say you need to earn two sales today, and you know, from a statistical standpoint, that on average it takes five presentations to do it.

Are you going to gear yourself to do only two presentations? Of course not. You'll expect to do five, and even if it takes six or seven to reach your quota, you should be prepared to do that many.

If you adopt the mentality that "this is too hard" or "this job takes too much effort," you'll only demotivate and disable yourself. Prepare instead to do whatever it takes to succeed—that is, make a large number of efforts—and you won't be disappointed. In fact, it will make success seem easier, because you were prepared to secure it the hard way if necessary.

The Formula for Success

Earlier I mentioned that Thomas Edison, perhaps the greatest inventor of all time, failed to perfect the incandescent light bulb some 10,000 times before succeeding. This is a great example of working HARD and SMART at the same time.

You've heard the adage that success is a matter of 1 percent inspiration and 99 percent perspiration, haven't you? This is yet another large-numbers insight. If Edison hadn't committed to working hard, he would not have succeeded with his inventions. I know this is true from personal experience.

The Principle of Inertia

One of the laws of thermodynamics says that a body in motion will tend to stay in motion, while a body at rest will tend to stay at rest. This applies to achieving success as well.

When I'm immersed in a consulting project, or I'm writing a book or designing a seminar, I find it much easier to finish unrelated projects during the same time period. When I have fewer significant projects to do, it seems really challenging to initiate or to finish anything.

I'm sure you're the same way. We might gripe because we're moving at the speed of light, trying to accomplish a lot of things. But this momentum enables us to produce disproportionate results.

If we slow down, we'll tend to slow down even more, until we don't have enough to do.

When You're Hot, You're Hot

Have you ever wondered why success seems to run in streaks? Why is it that our favorite sports teams will usually seem to have runs of good or bad luck? All of their players' injuries will seem to bunch up at a given time. Or they'll have a series of games in which they'll score lots of runs or points, only to cool off a few days later and not get on the scoreboard at all.

We know if we flip a coin 100 times, the odds are that heads will come up fifty times, and tails will appear the other fifty. But we also know that average distributions like this only occur *on average*. The rest of the time, wins seem to significantly outnumber losses, or the reverse.

In human terms, this means that we need to apply a large-numbers philosophy consistently. When we're hot, we should maximize our gains and keep adding wins as long as we can. And when we're not, we should keep moving forward so we'll get back into the winning column as soon as possible.

Success Breeds Success

Why do some people seem to succeed time after time, while others seem to fail with the same regularity? Are the former luckier or more talented, or is there something else at work?

Winners expect to win, and losers expect to lose.

Take a coach who has had a great deal of success with a team that is known to have great players. His reputation will enable him to jump teams, and he'll get hired at a premium salary by a team that isn't performing well. Typically he'll take his new team, even if it has inferior players, to greater heights than they would have achieved in his absence.

His skills will play a part in this outcome. But he will also relentlessly communicate his consistent expectation of winning to his new players. He won't accept defeat, except as a very temporary condition.

If you think I'm kidding, just remember what Dusty Baker achieved in his first year with the Chicago Cubs, after having made a consistent winner of the San Francisco Giants. If not for a foul-ball-grabbing fan, the Cubs might have made it all the way to the World Series (which they finally did in 2016).

Everybody Loves a Lover

Who are some of the most attractive people in the world? Ask a single person, and they'll say, "Those who are already taken!"

It's true, because many of these unavailable people exude self-confidence. Every day, by being in one relationship or more, they feel they are desirable, and having proven this to themselves, it appears obvious to others, who tend to believe it as well.

If we doubt our desirability, that's communicated too.

So, oddly, relationship-committed people seem to attract numerous overtures that they couldn't possibly pursue, while the uncommitted seem to garner relatively few.

Mating and dating gurus say that appearing unneedy and unavailable will increase your overall desirability. After all, to seem so pleasantly disinterested, you must have something going for you, right? And the more often others seem to be attracted to you, the more your belief that you are desirable is reinforced. So large numbers of positive responses elicit larger numbers still.

The Rich Get Rich and the Poor Get Poorer

Again, we see the power of momentum and large numbers working to create both wealth and misfortune.

As I write these words, more Americans have slipped below the official poverty level than ever before. At the same time, we can boast having more millionaires and billionaires than any other country.

When I was traveling on business, I met two entrepreneurs who specialize in purchasing apartment buildings. They were very forthcoming with me, and I learned a lot, especially about their large-numbers thinking. I mentioned that I might be interested in owning a small building someday, consisting of perhaps six units.

They instantly advised against it. "Try to find at least a fourteen-unit building," they said.

I asked them how they arrived at that number.

"At fourteen units, it makes sense to have an on-site manager, who can supervise the property and handle your rentals for you. It will be much more profitable for you."

I asked them how many units they owned.

"Fifteen thousand," they replied smoothly. And they were still growing.

You Can't Predict Who Will Say Yes

When I was a young manager, I assigned territories to salespeople. Almost without fail, each one would plead for a great area and a really good list of prospects to call on.

I'd reply with my standard statement, "There's no such thing as a great list—only great salespeople!" They'd moan at first, but then they'd carry on, which is what I wanted them to do.

No matter how experienced we are in business, it's hard to avoid trying to predict who will say yes or no. It's a game that we play with ourselves. But unlike a mere game, guessing like this has significant consequences.

Let me give you an example. I agreed to do a seminar under the sponsorship of a large university. The person I dealt with was friendly and professional, and our negotiations went very smoothly. But if you had asked me a week ago if I thought we were going to get anywhere, the answer would have been no. How come?

I prejudged her on the basis of her name and her voice-mail message. Both seemed stodgy and stuffy to me. In fact, when I first chatted with her, she seemed exactly this way. But almost immediately, she loosened up, defying my prejudgment, and happily so.

Contact Your Entire List

When I was attending college, I sold advertising on a part-time basis. One day I closed a deal with the owner of a marine supply store.

When I turned in my sales at the end of the shift, the boss breathlessly asked me if I had really made that sale. He couldn't believe it. "That guy is so tight he squeaks," he said.

Apparently that one sale made me the most credible salesman in the world, at least in his eyes. If he had seen my list in advance, he probably would have waved me away from the deal, saying, "Oh, forget about that one. I know him."

There is a moral to this story. Whether you're in sales or not, contact your entire list. No one is psychic enough to know in advance who isn't worth contacting. If they could pick winners beforehand, they'd have no business being in business. They'd be better off at the racetrack.

Repeat Large-Numbers Affirmations

I'm urging you to employ a large-numbers mentality, and if this is new to you, it will feel strange. It will take practice to master. Furthermore, your interest going to flag from time to time.

What can I do to help you to stay on the right path? I believe the answer rests in providing you with affirmative statements that you can repeat weekly or daily. Here are some of my favorites.

I will not stop, hesitate, or be deterred!

Some of the strongest people I know repeat this mantra before facing life's toughest challenges. It makes them nothing less than invincible.

The entire idea of a large-numbers commitment is to carry on long past the time at which others might have quit. Like that battery-powered bunny on TV, your wins will come after you have decided to go on, and on, and on, and on.

One monkey doesn't stop the show.

Nobody enjoys hearing personal criticism or negative feedback, but there will always be detractors who will revel in sending it your way. Their purpose isn't constructive. It's to knock you down. If they can, they'll go for a knockout and try to make you stay down for the count.

Remind yourself that one monkey doesn't stop the show. Never, ever make one person's feedback or opinion matter so much that it retards your progress. If you need to, rebut the criticism or discount it at the first chance you get. If there's a grain of truth in what they said, accept only a grain's worth of the rebuke and then go on with your work.

I will persist long after lesser souls would have quit.

Make persistence your specialty. Tell yourself, when the going gets tough, the tough get going. Be one of the people who will never say die.

In fact, think of your job description and your life's mission as persisting, come what may. You might be a plumber, a lawyer, or a schoolteacher, but your real responsibility is persisting. Think, "I'm a persistor!"

I don't care how many nos I get,
it's the yesses that count.

Invent your own math of success. It may take 1000 resumes to get a single job interview. So what? That's why copy machines were invented—to mass-produce the written word! If the job you get after sending out those thousand resumes, makes you happy, pays you well, and gives you a positive outlook, it has been worth every ounce of your effort to get—right? Even if it offers temporary relief from unemployment, it's still a step up.

My Dad used to say, "It only takes one" when he'd cheer me on at my baseball games. He realized that I might have to look at a number of pitches, but it only took a single one that I could hit to make all the difference in my game.

Maybe I'm not experiencing enough rejections!

When I was in grade school, I used to devour biographies of our nation's presidents and other leaders. I recall coming across a particularly vivid portrait of Senator Thomas Hart Benton. He considered himself a tough guy, and to prove the point he claimed that he burnished his skin regularly with a horsehair brush. Imagine wanting to be so tough that you would purposely put yourself through such treatments!

Could it be that we avoid disappointments and rejection so much that we don't garner enough to become inured to the stuff? Might it be better if we actually put ourselves into the position of being rebuffed more often?

Think about what you've been avoiding and why. Would you achieve more self-confidence by confronting it directly? Perhaps this is what people mean when they say we should do what we fear.

Here's to Good Days and to Better Ones!

Let's make a toast to good days and to better ones. I admire what I heard an older gentleman say: every day above ground is a good day!

As Buddhists suggest, at every moment we have a chance to wake up, to become enlightened. We can use whatever is happening to us at the moment to accomplish this noble result. Even if we're in pain or suffering through depression, according to author and nun Pema Chödrön, we have a shot at attaining enlightenment. We can make friends with our situation, no matter how uncomfortable it is.

In this sense, every day and even each moment is a good one. It may not be as peaceful or as warm and comforting as a day at the beach, but it is still good and worthwhile.

People who are in great pain, or who are meeting their deaths after being ill, are often especially aware of the value of each moment. They may not have many days or weeks or months left. But they do have an astonishing number of moments, each of which can bring fresh perception, appreciation, and understanding.

Right now we can revel in the fact that if we *are* healthy, we may be blessed with the prospects of enjoying a million or more seconds, each or any of which can bring us joy. Just knowing that *this* might become our most glorious or clear-sighted second can set us free. We always foster that sort of potential, just as the acorn fosters the great oak inside. We can make more of our future than we have of the past, even if it seems that, by conventional measures, we have less ahead of us than we have behind.

Large-numbers thinking says more than that the glass is half-full. It says we should appreciate and recognize each drop that is in the glass. As we look closer and closer at anything, we see more of what is really there. Like the atom, which when harnessed or split contains huge powers, our abilities to outdo ourselves are intertwined with the smallest of details. All we have to do is pay more attention to them, and we'll multiply our possibilities, and our happiness.

So here's to good days and to better ones! And here's to the briefest of moments and the tiniest of details. They are all worth multiplying and relishing.

The Limits of Your Language Are the Limits of Your World

It has probably been some time since you've given any thought to the size of your vocabulary. But at least one linguist is convinced that the limits of your language are the limits of your world. If you don't have a word to describe something, it won't exist for you in the same way as it does for someone who does.

A good example can be found in the movie *Smilla's Sense of Snow*. Smilla is a character who grew up in Greenland, where there is a lot of snow. In fact there are all kinds of snow, with differing hues, textures, and so forth. Smilla has a vast knowledge of snow, so after the death of a child who was found in the snow, she was called on to use her knowledge to figure out how he met his demise. The result is a taut mystery and a very interesting insight into how perceptual abilities differ among people.

Do yourself a favor. Pick up the dictionary and read a few pages. Take extra time to read definitions of words you never learned. You'll be amazed by how interesting an adventure this will become for you.

Do the same thing with a neat reference book that is a staple in the libraries of professional speakers: *Bartlett's Familiar Quotations*. You'll see who originally said some of your favorite things, and you'll also be able to read some of the greatest ideas ever expressed, in a nutshell.

Both of these sources will improve your brain power and multiply your ability to appreciate nuances. You'll also expand your capacity to express yourself in new ways.

Avoid Hardening of the Attitudes

As we mature, it's tempting to experience a certain hardening of our attitudes. After all, they seem to have brought us to where we are today, so why not keep seeing things as we've seen them before?

Actually, we should be doing the opposite. We should actively seek new perspectives and broaden our worlds.

For instance, I ran across a book that purports to show the reader how to see things. Most us were born with an operational sense of sight, so what contribution could a book like this make? We can see already, can't we? But that's the point. We look, and sometimes we gaze, but we don't *see* very much at all.

Let's say you venture forth to a coffee shop to order a drink. You'll scan the parking lot for a space, and once inside, you'll check out where to line up to place your order. You may or may not see the menu on the wall or pay attention to the prices next to the items listed. And there are many things you probably won't pay attention to at all.

What's the color scheme? I'm sitting in a coffee shop as I write this, and I can see that there is a theme. It's brown, like coffee, but there are dashes of green and accents of orange as well. The servers are wearing orange baseball caps, and the posters on the wall also mirror the brown and orange theme.

Next I'm going to look at the vertical elements of the place. There are lamps that hang low over the counters; also there are some wrought-iron bins on the counters that contain toffees and other sweets. I've never paid any attention to them before.

I could focus on the sounds of the place, or the pace at which customers or servers move, or any of dozens of separate but related dimensions of this experience. Having so many options, how could I ever grow bored or even impatient? The constantly changing mix of people, along with their conversations, clothing, gestures, tones, and the like, means that there is an incredible amount of stimulation here. Moreover, I could make this an even richer experience by asking whether these design elements are pleasant or unpleasant, or as effective as they could be. I could spend hours and hours checking this place out without exhausting the possibilities for exploration. Just when you've seen it all, there's even more to be seen!

Multiply Your Appreciations

It stands to reason that with the more details you see, the more you have to appreciate at a given time.

It can get us down emotionally when we forget to appreciate, or think that we have less and less to appreciate. If you deliberately list all of your actual or potential enjoyments at a given time, you'll have more and more reasons to rejoice.

Just take a moment to watch a grandparent as they observe their children's children at play. You can see that they revel in each moment, trying not to miss the hint of a smile or frown, or the emergence of a new skill or interest.

No detail is too small, and no moment is too fleeting that it isn't given its proper acknowledgement and appreciation. Don't wait to be a grandma or grandpa to experience life in its richest details.

Ask at Least One Interesting Question

I have a great time satisfying my curiosity. One of the best ways of doing it is by interviewing people. It's amazing to me how people will open up to us if we're genuinely interested in them. Even famous people, I've found, will give you a meaningful reply if you ask a high-quality question.

I've always admired author Ray Bradbury. In graduate school, I wrote a paper or two about his novel *Fahrenheit 451* and the film made from it. I always wondered how he felt about the movie in light of the fact that it departed somewhat from his book.

Once, when I was strolling in Beverly Hills, I stood next to the gentleman at a traffic signal. Within second of recognizing him, I asked him what he thought of the film.

"It brought me to tears," he replied.

That's exactly what it did to me, and it was great to share that feeling with the author himself.

Likewise, I ran into investment guru Peter Lynch at the Honolulu airport recently. I asked him if he still liked stocks, especially in what was a so-so market, and he replied, "I always like stocks!" It was an enjoyable exchange. Naturally I interpreted his reply as a buy signal, and I profited from acting on it.

What would *you* like to know, and who knows it? Reach out to them, and you'll be rewarded with very interesting and helpful replies.

Inch by Inch, It's a Cinch

If you're ever feeling overwhelmed by a challenge, break down the solution into small steps. You'll find that there is always something you can do, however modest or minor, that will enable you to create some positive forward movement.

Then, when you have racked up a minor victory, you will feel motivated to add to it. Before long, you'll have a string of wins that will add up to a mighty achievement.

For instance, when I get an idea for a new seminar, I'll initially experience a surge of excitement. I might shop the idea to some friends and colleagues to hear what they think of it.

But even if I receive positive feedback, I'll feel a pit in my stomach, because I'll realize that having an idea and executing it well are very different things. However, I know from experience that I'll need to do something tangible to bring the class into existence. For me, it's composing a course description.

If I can put something together that seems compelling, I will have taken a very big step. It might take only an hour or a half day to do, but it will often be sufficient to shop around to potential sponsors. Then I'll outline the course, and create the individual units that will serve as its ultimate content.

Put Yourself at Cause

At any point in our lives, we are either *at cause* or *at effect*. The difference involves much more than semantics. It informs the very quality of our lives and our sense of vitality.

People who are at cause feel that they're in charge of the events that unfold before them. To a large extent, they're right.

It's very much like what the designer, Coco Chanel, retorted to a Parisian passerby who asserted, "What you're wearing is out of style!"

Chanel shot back, "I *make* style."

I love that story because it typifies the confidence that at-cause people feel. They make style in their own worlds. They don't need to follow anyone's limiting definitions of how they should look, act, or feel. They make such determinations for themselves, and many at-cause people are the trendsetters for millions of others.

When I was in law school, I was already an accomplished writer and consultant. When we were asked to introduce ourselves at the beginning of the first year's class, I mentioned that I had published some books.

Snippily the professor asked, "What kind of author are you?"

"Best-selling," I replied.

He never asked me another tainted question about my background.

I also recall a time when I was making an impassioned argument about a case in a torts class. The professor wanted to impeach my credibility, so he asked, "On what authority do you make that argument?"

"On my own authority," I responded.

These may seem like cocky rejoinders, and perhaps they were. But you have to feel your fundamental right to make them. You have to be at cause.

What made me so confident? I had achieved enough references to feel I had earned the right to proudly be me. In the first case, I *had* written some best-sellers, and in the second, I was used to making my own interpretations of facts because I was a PhD—a trained thinker.

A Small-Numbers Outlook
Will Put You at Effect

When you're at effect, the world seems to be constantly having its way with you. Instead of being a mover and shaker, you're the moved and the shaken. You feel as if you're always taking orders and executing other people's agendas. If life were one grand party, you'd be the valet who was parking cars for everybody else. Instead of being seated at the feast, you'd be lucky to score a doggy bag of scraps to take home after your exhausting shift.

A sure way to feel at effect is to allow a small-numbers mind-set to take hold of you. Once you feel your outlook is narrowing and your options shrinking, you're at effect.

Growing older can do the trick for many. Because they associate youth with having vitality and relatively unlimited choices, many aging people believe, wrongly, that their vistas must shrink. Conversely, there are plenty of young people who think that the odds of success are against them because they don't have much experience.

Either perception is problematic and should be actively disputed.

Watch Out for Limiting Generalizations

Listen to what your inner voice is feeding your unconscious. Do you hear it issuing limiting generalizations? Here are some typical ones:

- *I'll never be any good at this!*
- *I always seem to screw this up!*
- *I absolutely must succeed this time!*
- *I'll only do this one more time, then I give up!*
- *You have to have special gifts to get good at this!*

What do all of these generalizations have in common? They lack proof.

"I'll Never Be Good at This!"

Take the first one—that you'll never be any good at something. How can you tell at this point? Aren't you being a little hasty in making this judgment?

If there's one thing that I've learned from being in the martial arts, it is that I can master any move. All I have to do is allow myself enough time.

That, of course, is a large-numbers proposition. During the time I allow, naturally I'll try and try again. What's more, I'll keep trying until I get it right. And when I have mastered what used to be an impossible move, I feel elated, but I also feel that it was easier to get than I thought it would be.

"I Always Seem to Screw This Up!"

Are you a *total* screwup? I doubt it. Again, you're probably generalizing. There have to be certain aspects of any process that you're doing perfectly well.

For instance, you may be a writer who seems to be blocked. You're staring at your blank computer screen. What have you done right so far?

Hey, you sat down and turned on the machine. You cordoned off some time in order to write. All that has to happen next is for you to suspect your generalizations long enough to let some words *of whatever quality* come out.

As I write these words, by the way, I'm having a great time. But only two days ago, I had to force myself to get under way. I don't think you'll be able to detect the difference in my work product, though.

"I Absolutely Must Succeed This Time!"

Who says you *absolutely must* succeed, and succeed *this time*? In fact, who is saying you absolutely *must* do anything?

You are. Why are you telling yourself this claptrap?

Don't answer that, at least not right now. You don't need to answer it, except by disputing it. Disputing weakens its power and enables you to make forward progress. Why not allow yourself innumerable times to get it right? Wouldn't that relieve the pressure to perform, which is self-imposed anyway?

If you feel the need to limit your attempts, pick a large number. Imagine how good you would get at putting golf balls or serving tennis balls if you committed to doing it, say, a hundred times per outing.

Sportscaster Vin Scully rejoiced in telling us how Todd Helton, slugger with the Colorado Rockies, became such a great hitter. "His dad built him a batting cage, and young Todd swung at balls until his hands bled," beamed Vin.

Obviously Scully was a large-numbers fan.

Just for fun, imagine what kind of hitter Helton would have become if he had limited his batting practice to hitting, say, ten pitches during each outing. Would his batting eye, his timing, his coordination, or his power be anything like what they became with more numerous efforts?

No way!

"I'll Only Do This One More Time, Then I Give Up!"

When I jog, I don't allow myself to envision the finishing line. If I do, I start to feel fatigued. My performance from that point feels as if it is all uphill.

Don't even think of quitting.

Be generous with yourself. Tell yourself that sooner or later, success will come your way. Even if it's tardy, or it is a no-show, your character will be stronger for your unwavering commitment.

"You Have to Have Special Gifts to Get Good at This!"

When I was starting my martial-arts training, I was awed and amazed by the prowess of senior belts. They did everything with so much speed, power, and elegance.

One fellow in particular was really smooth. He looked like a professional dancer. Every move was distinctive, yet when he put them together, they flowed like a mighty stream.

I remember thinking a lot of limiting thoughts. "You have to have special gifts of coordination and athleticism to master this stuff!" was one. "It helps if you're a dancer or an acrobat or gymnast," I also mused.

I was putting myself at effect with these dumb assertions. Now, after seven years of hard work, I look a lot like him when he moved. I've mastered the aesthetic.

Does he still look better than I do? Of course—he's in his twelfth year, I believe.

The only difference now is that I know I'll be able to keep up with him, and still outdo my personal best, providing I keep trying and I don't disable myself with any more stupid generalizations.

"Every Day, in Every Way, I'm Getting Better and Better!"

Imagine what would happen if we asserted the opposite generalizations.

For instance, what would your performance be like if you told yourself, "Every day, in every way, I'm getting better and better?"

This is the exact wording that pioneering psychologist Émile Coué would have his patients repeat to intensify their feelings of well-being while heightening their achievements.

If you're in a cynical mood, you might retort, "That's a generalization too, isn't it?"

You'd be correct, but it is more constructive to endorse this idea than its opposite, wouldn't you agree?

By the way, Coué's declaration is a mighty antidote to the poison that elders put into their minds saying they are rapidly declining. If the Bible is right in saying, "As you think, so you are," then we would all be wise to think we're improving more and more.

The Patience of Surfers

When I visited San Diego's Coronado Island and then Hawaii, I took some surfing lessons. Naturally I was clumsy at first, but I was able to catch some waves, and I ended up having a blast.

I'm watching surfers right now as I gaze out my living-room window. I feel I'm getting to know them in an unconventional way. One thing I see is their incredible patience.

Today the surf is anything but up. The swells are small, and the sets seem to be few and far between. Nonetheless, there are two dozen riders in view who are placidly waiting for their next chance to catch a wave. The average surfer is waiting about five minutes to have anything to paddle into. Then it takes an average of three attempts to catch a wave that one tries for. So every fifteen minutes, the typical enthusiast rides one.

To me, as a very occasional participant, this doesn't seem to be all that much fun.

Catching four waves per hour isn't very many. Add to this the fact that most rides seem to last for less than three seconds, and you're talking about twelve seconds of fun every sixty minutes.

There are 3600 seconds in every hour, so .00333, or a little more the 3/1000 of the total time in the water, consists of wave riding, which is the goal of surfing. The remaining time entails waiting for waves and attempting to catch them.

Yet surfing can be one of the most exciting sports. Why is there such an apparent disconnection between the patience, effort, and time invested and the total return in actual performance? It takes large numbers simply to come away with a minimal surfing experience, yet it is still enjoyable, and for most, it certainly beats a day at the office.

I think the answer is counterintuitive. Most of us assume that we need lots of positive reinforcement to feel that we're good at something and that it is enjoyable. Surfers demonstrate a willingness to forgo frequent reinforcements. They'll settle for the occasional one, possibly because the enjoyment they get from it is still emotionally proportionate to their investment.

I suspect seasoned surfers really don't count their wipeouts, or the missed waves, or the overall time in the water, unless they're on a tight schedule. They measure the total value of the experience.

Gazing at a limitless horizon, unimpeded by buildings, cars, and people, is really very enjoyable. The uncertainly ushered in by whether you will or won't catch a wave can be exhilarating. And not knowing how long a ride can be made to last is also very appealing, because it too is a happy variable that keeps you interested in the activity.

Surfers also know that they constitute a breed apart. No one can surf with ease and poise unless they too make a large-numbers investment. If you're willing to pay this price, then you can join a fairly exclusive club.

No Pain, No Gain

Speaking as an athlete who enjoys karate, running, weight training, and just about any activity that involves throwing, kicking, or catching a spherical or oblong object, I can say this: the conditioning that it takes to prepare for the sport is a big part of the fun. There is actual joy in the phrase "No pain, no gain."

You know that you're willing to pay the price of achieving victory, and this fact makes you part of an elite. Before bodybuilding became so popular, people used to snicker, "Why would anyone want to get that big and muscular?"

One answer is that they *can* if they try hard. And if they try the hardest, they can become the biggest, and yes, set records and become legends, just as Arnold Schwarzenegger did.

They have to be willing to work through the pain of doing the largest numbers. If they're weight training, they do more repetitions, more sets, and consistently add more weight.

I've already mentioned that Todd Helton took practiced batting until his hands bled. Putting in such efforts, sustaining occasional injuries, and recovering from setbacks, *increases* the enjoyment and appreciation of the sport.

Many of us simply don't respect what comes easily. Vince Lombardi said that there is something inside of true competitors that makes them "love the grind." They get a thrill from leaving "the field of battle exhausted, but victorious," as Lombardi pointed out.

The Desire to Win Is Nothing without the Desire to Prepare!

A number of years ago, Robert Pirsig wrote a novel called *Zen and the Art of Motorcycle Maintenance*. It tells the story of a cross-country motorcycle trip that the narrator took with his son.

But the book is really a deep exploration of what constitutes "quality." Pirsig asks whether quality is subjective or objective. He wonders whether it is something inherent in an object or a machine, or something positive that people derive from using it. Finally, he seems to conclude that quality involves *caring*. Typically, when you care about building or fixing a motorcycle, or anything for that matter, you do a better job of it than when you just try to rush through the process and get it over with.

Quality is the coming together of desire and skill, the two halves of the brain, rationality and spirituality.

When we are committed to achieving quality, a certain peace accompanies our work and play, and we can whole-heartedly do whatever it takes to achieve positive results.

Pirsig's book serves as a reminder that the desire to win must be accompanied by the desire to prepare. We need to teach our kids and ourselves to appreciate the process of doing something instead of obsessing about getting immediate or easy results.

A large-numbers philosophy contributes to creating a quality frame of mind, whether we're surfing, weight training, or repairing machines. When we start with a committed attitude, our achievements inevitably reflect it, and we can then rightly say they have quality.

Want More Oil? Dig More Wells

Recently there was a scandal involving a giant multi-national oil company. Apparently it had overstated the amount of proven reserves of crude oil in the ground.

Over the years, oil firms have extracted more oil in part by digging more deeply into existing wells. Techno-logical advances in equipment and computer modeling have enabled them to tap into additional deposits.

But now there is some doubt that added reserves, even if they exist, can be extracted without bringing up a huge amount of water at the same time, thus diluting the value of the crude component.

I find this very interesting, because I distinctly remember hearing the old adage that if you want more oil, you'll need to dig more holes. It's ironic that this large-numbers assertion seems as true today as it was when it was first coined.

Whenever you sense that your reserves of cash, opportunities, enjoyments, or enthusiasm are dwindling, as yourself:

Am I digging enough wells, or am I kidding myself that I'll improve my circumstances by staying in the holes I'm already in?

Self-Discipline through Large Numbers

In another section, I mentioned that a large-numbers viewpoint can be seen in numerous virtues. I mentioned that it takes some perseverance to overcome our tendency to cut and run and settle for having small-numbers experiences.

There is a kindred virtue that we need to recognize as an essential part of the scheme. It is SELF-DISCIPLINE.

Once I was consulting for a former Marine who had become an entrepreneur. I was observing him as he trained his salespeople. At a crucial moment he barked: *"Discipline is the most important thing in life!"*

I thought he may have been overstating the point, but as I've matured and witnessed my own highs and lows in achievement, I'm giving it more weight. Let me put it this way: self-discipline is one of the most important virtues that you can cultivate.

By committing yourself to implement the wisdom of the Law of Large Numbers, you'll be exerting self-discipline.

Fulfilling the grunt work of doing things repeatedly will increase your store of self-discipline, enabling you to take on even greater challenges.

"Nobody Ever Got Rich Selling Self-Discipline!"

I was watching a PBS program on obesity the other night, and a number of weight-loss program administrators were interviewed.

When one gentleman was asked whether all good programs really boil down to eating good things in smaller portions and exercising, he said that they do. But then he observed, "Nobody ever got rich by selling self-discipline."

So we see countless ads for quack diets and exercise machines that promise instant results with no sacrifices required. "Eat all you want of whatever you want" would be ideal, and it's what dieters want to hear.

"Never exercise again!" is another attractive lure. But inside we know that we have to do certain things differently if we want to achieve better results.

Producing change and staying the same cancel each other out. However, I disagree with the gentleman who said nobody gets rich by selling self-discipline. Perhaps that's valid if we're trying to sell miracle cures or diets.

Most of the people I know who have grown wealthy have done it by selling self-discipline to themselves.

This is the key. The Marine sold himself on the virtue of being disciplined and made it a pivotal part of his philosophy of life. He grew a company through discipline, and he grew rich. If we were to examine how he put discipline into practice, it would appear as several large-numbers commitments and performances.

"Sure, It Was Hard, but You Did It Hard!"

If we're lucky, at some point we'll wake up and understand that we're simply going to have to do things the hard way. If we want success, a great mate, dear friends, if we want to serve others and get the most from life, we'll need to exert continuous effort.

When I was seventeen and about to graduate from high school, my older brother sat me down for a heart-to-heart talk. He said that nothing in life was going to be handed to me. There wouldn't be any money available for higher education, and if I wanted to attend, I'd have to go to put myself through community college first, and then work my way through the ranks to a four-year public university.

I didn't like hearing this. But something deep within me knew he was on the level. I'd have to do everything the hard way if I wanted to make any kind of life for myself. I resolved to buckle down and get the job done. Working at a succession of menial full-time jobs, I rented a one-room apartment and went to school full-time.

Motivational speaker Les Brown puts it this way: "Sure it was hard. But you did it hard!"

I love that statement, because it sums up the attitude you need to get the most from the large-numbers idea.

You need to be prepared to do it hard, to do it relentlessly, to do it come what may. And what is the "it" that you need to do?

You need to do YOUR THING, whatever you decide it is.

Ambivalence Is Your Enemy

Recently I read a book that said that some people work very hard climbing the ladder of success only to find later on that it was leaning against the wrong wall. In other words, they chose the wrong goal.

This can happen, I suppose, but for some the goal was perfectly fine when they started their ascent. It was simply no longer relevant to their needs by the time they reached the top.

I believe a more profound problem is not having a clear goal to begin with. Or having too many goals, or fostering goals that conflict with one another.

For instance, I ran a seminar where one participant wore about five hats. She was involved in real estate, tax preparation, personal fitness training, and a few other endeavors. She sensed that she needed to focus, but I could detect that she was really not energized about any one thing that he did. After a lot of probing, the fact came out that she really longed to travel. The fix seemed to be refocusing her business interests so they would facilitate instead of hindering her ability to get away. Once she saw that, she was reenergized.

We need to clarify our goals in order to feel free to throw ourselves into a large-numbers campaign. If we don't, we'll stop short of achieving substantial results.

You Can Set Goals Even if They're Not Clear

Today I was discussing the large-numbers concept with a friend, and he asked me if it was essential to have clear-cut goals before inaugurating a campaign.

After thinking about it for a few minutes, I decided it is helpful to have clear goals, but not essential. I gave the example of a person who serves drinks at a coffee bar.

I said that she could commit to cleaning more tables more efficiently and more completely than anybody else on the crew. It wouldn't be a major life goal certainly, but it would be a small objective.

Although this campaign didn't appear to provide any real victory, I went on to postulate that some really exciting things could result from it. First, the server's manager could see that she was dedicated to achieving results in a very unglamorous occupation. Her dedication, hard work, and self-starting qualities would shine through. She would become clearly distinguishable from her less energetic peers. Before long, she would elevate herself into a whole new class or category. It would be a category of one—she would be its sole occupant. Whenever new opportunities or positions opened up, she would leap several steps on the ladder of consideration.

But what if she had no ambitions at the coffee bar? What would she achieve? She'd build equity towards earning a great job reference. She'd get into the habit of working hard, which would serve her everywhere. Plus, she could exalt in the feeling that she was the very best at doing her job.

Large Numbers and Your Personality

The other day I was listening to a consultant complain about what he felt he had to do to generate business. He said, "I hate networking and all of that glad-handing that goes with it, but I'm pretty good at it, I suppose, and it does bring in business." He went on to say that he preferred to get add-on business from his current clients, as well as referrals from them.

Well, duh, I thought. Who doesn't enjoy passively harvesting the low-lying fruit? It doesn't require us to reach very far, or to even break a sweat. It's always more arduous to plant new trees, to lose many of them as saplings, and to nurse the survivors along until they too bear fruit. Relative to picking fruit from mature orchards, going through the entire cycle is always a pain.

But he didn't want the pain. The pleasure was fine, but not the pain.

When I suggested that he consider asking more of his current clients for additional business, he balked and replied, "Well, I don't want to seem too aggressive."

He didn't want to hear it, but I told him there was no avoiding the discomfort. The good news is that by asking more, he'll receive more, and he will become a stronger person for having gone through the ordeal. It will strengthen his personality. Instead of being threatened by rejection, his ego will be fortified, and he'll find he is increasingly capable in the future.

If You Want Rainbows, You'll Have to Put Up with the Rain

As you know, the government to some extent regulates the claims that can be made in advertising. I wonder what would happen if suddenly no further references could be made to something being easy.

Instantly all of those fad diets would be in jeopardy. They're always touting how easy it is to lose weight if you simply binge on pineapple, or cut out carbohydrates, or eat your way thin. Exercise equipment makers couldn't tell us how easy it is to climb electronic stairs or work out our abdominal muscles. And those who suggest that we'll only have to make so many easy payments would be stuck and have to search for other adjectives to woo us into buying.

If we got rid of the word *easy*, might we become more realistic in accepting that everything useful, desirable, and even different usually requires that we either forbear from pleasure or accept certain levels of discomfort?

Would we appreciate, as singer Dolly Parton once observed, "If you want rainbows, you have to put up with the rain"?

We Don't Solve Most of Our Problems; We Outlive Them

One of my mentors, Professor Peter Drucker, is renowned for his insights in the field of management, but he also had some keen insights into human nature. He observed that we don't solve many of our thorniest problems. Instead, if we're lucky, we'll outlive them. In other words, they'll simply become less relevant or important with the passage of time.

I've seen already this in my life. Once I was obsessed with succeeding right away with everything. If there was any activity in which I didn't show instant prowess, I was turned off to it.

Now I appreciate that I was suffering from low frustration tolerance. Instead of expecting instant gratification, I appreciate that many of our most significant endeavors take incredible commitments to achieve.

Are Deadlines Necessary?

When I first studied management by objectives, I learned that goal-setting wasn't sufficient to produce predictable and reliable business outcomes. Too often goals were really like wishes. We hoped they would come true, but we made no comprehensive plans for making them come true.

An objective is often defined as a goal with a deadline attached. It is a commitment to achieve something specific by a certain date. It has four dimensions: quality, quantity, cost, and time.

For instance, I might set an objective of becoming wealthy. It becomes an actionable objective when I spell it out this way:

I will earn $10 million by December 31, 2023. I will achieve this by building my speaking, consulting, and publishing enterprises.

That's fairly concrete, isn't it?

By introducing a deadline, I'm trying to create accountability. I should be able to see how much I'm on track at any point between now and 12-31-2023.

There are a lot of constructive aspects to objectives and to the deadlines they introduce. But are they always necessary, or even constructive?

Let's say you want to improve your golf handicap. Must you introduce a deadline for it? Unless you're a pro, I would think that such a goal would make you more tense and less likely to enjoy yourself, let alone lowering that handicap.

Shouldn't you be willing to work toward your goal for as long as it takes to achieve it? Let's say you set this objective:

I will lower my handicap to 68, and I will enjoy the process of doing it, no matter how long it takes, whether I seem to be making progress or not.

Could we change the wealth-seeking objective in the same manner? How's this?

I will earn ten million dollars and achieve it by using any honest and gratifying means.

That's pretty open-ended, I admit. But in some ways, isn't it more realistic, and doesn't it feel more comfortable, from the get-go?

Reconsider the wisdom in some of the deadlines you've set for yourself. Are they helping you, or are they merely introducing undesirable anxiety and stress?

Getting back to those fad diets, note how many of them contain testimonials such as, "I lost 6000 pounds in six weeks!" Not only are they claiming it's easy, but they're also asserting that it's quick.

Large-numbers advocates don't need either inducement to achieve. In fact we're perfectly comfortable telling ourselves that we'll get results, no matter how hard it is, and no matter how long it takes.

Knowing this, we can feel free to enjoy the process.

Science Leaps Forward
by Riding Lots of Horses

Recently I had the opportunity to consult for some very sharp people, one of whom is a research scientist. We talked about the Law, and he mentioned that in his field, research endeavors are often tacitly informed by it. A dozen scientists in a lab might be looking at a disease, but each one is assigned to examining a different aspect of it. The director of the lab knows that sooner or later one of the horses in his stable will win the Triple Crown, as my contact put it.

Some research leaders are luckier than others in identifying rewarding areas, just as some people are better at handicapping the ponies at the racetrack. But there is a direct correlation between the number of horses you have running in the race and your chances of winning, and winning big.

"All you need is one winner every so often," the researcher said, "and your funding and your career are set."

I'm sure the same large-numbers deployment of scientists can be seen in pharmaceutical companies that every now and then devise blockbuster drugs.

"Colleges Are Very Successful, but They Don't Know It"

When I was speaking at universities, I had a chance to pick the brain of a fellow who had devised a very successful seminar enterprise of his own. In many subject areas, he competed directly with colleges, so he had a very interesting perspective on their strengths and weaknesses.

He said colleges were quite good at delivering quality seminars, but they were not nearly as capable when it came to promoting them. He said, "They don't mail enough brochures to make courses as profitable as they can be."

He went on to note that colleges might achieve a 5 percent return on their mailers, so for every 100 they would send, they'd sign up five people. The problem was that they'd only mail 300 for each class, and they'd squeak by with fifteen participants.

"They should mail ten times as many as they do, and they'd get an amazing return," he declared. In light of the fact that the average direct mail response was 1–2 percent, they were very successful, but they didn't know it. They needed to implement large-numbers thinking into their promotions.

Are You a Money Personality?

A few years ago, I found a very useful book, *The Money Personality*, by Dr. Sidney Lecker. He points out that certain people are more likely to amass wealth if they highlight certain traits.

One of them is to be unafraid of bigness. Colleges didn't mail out enough flyers because, I suspect, they were afraid of the bigger apparent risks that would come with endorsing and then performing a large-numbers campaign.

Lecker says this kind of fear is stultifying, and if we foster it, we'll inhibit our capabilities. Instead we should understand that rewards go to the bold. We shouldn't stop short of achieving the success that we can enjoy if we extend our gains to their logical conclusions.

Lecker also says that money personalities don't suffer from money guilt, thinking that it is evil. They also come to appreciate that the bigger you are, the softer you'll fall if you suffer some losses.

Try to See the Big in the Small

I enjoy jogging almost daily at the beach. For the most part, my town is very good at keeping its open spaces free of debris and trash. But naturally there will be errant wrappers, cola cans, and other items that litter the area. So after I jog, I make it a point to reach down and pick up anywhere from one to five pieces of trash.

One day, when I did this, I noticed a jogger who ran in the opposite direction, and he followed my lead. Slowing down to a near-stop, he bent over, retrieved a piece of paper, and disposed of it in one graceful motion. Then he carried on with his run.

I know if I simply make this small gesture every day, I'll dispose of hundreds, if not a thousand or more, of these unsightly items each year. Over the course of a decade, it will add up to an enormous amount.

Helping the environment doesn't have to involve the government or a political group. You can do a lot all by yourself. It only requires a small gesture here and there, repeated consistently over time. It is a large-numbers campaign that is contained in a series of very modest motions.

Large-Numbers Campaigns
Are Habit-Forming

The Law urges us to do enough of anything, and we'll succeed. Do more than that, and we'll grow rich. Then do even more still, and we'll become legends.

As you move from stage to stage, you become accustomed to practicing large-numbers behaviors. You find that when you are getting into a bad mood, or a slump, or a depression, you only have to ask yourself where you're succumbing to a small-numbers mentality.

"What am I not doing that I should be doing more of?" becomes the guiding question.

Let's say you've broken up with a long-standing intimate. It's customary to recoil, lick one's wounds, and grieve for a period of time. Before too long, however, you need to get back out into the world.

The only thing that will reestablish your sense of vitality is reconnecting with people, and the more, the merrier. Inevitably, you'll find there are kindred spirits who enter your life who would otherwise not appear if you didn't force yourself to use a large-numbers approach.

You may be reluctant at first to get back into circulation. But by doing it, you'll find it becomes easier and easier to stay out there, and before long, it becomes a good habit that serves you well.

Reaching Enlightenment through the Law

According to Zen Buddhists, we are only steps away from achieving enlightenment, or a heightened awareness of life. Often those who seek enlightenment are treated to a large-numbers procedure to assist them in waking up.

Some Zen masters bombard their students with riddles, known as *koans*, that force them to suspend their habit of avoiding a here-and-now experience of reality. A second approach invites the student to quiet the mind by systematically reducing its cascading thoughts.

Both approaches involve large numbers.

Five Hundred Fights

In the movie *Knockaround Guys*, Vin Diesel's character strides up to a gangster in a bar, looks him in the eye, and flatly says, "Five hundred."

The gangster quips, "What's that supposed to mean?"

Diesel replies, "Five hundred street fights. That's what I figured it took before you could call yourself a legitimate tough guy."

At that moment, the gangster's face starts to register fear. Was Diesel telling him that he purposely fought 500 times to consider himself tough enough?

That's exactly what Diesel went on to say before he kicked the stuffing out of the gangster.

The scene is powerful because Diesel is calm and so self-assured. He knows he's tougher than the punk he's facing. But the punk needs to find out, not only by flailing fists, but by appreciating the price Diesel was willing to pay to achieve his tough-guy status.

What kind of person will intentionally put himself at risk 500 times to prove anything?

In your walk of life, given your hopes and dreams, are you willing to become that kind of large-numbers person?

"It's Not for Everyone"

I met a fellow writer a few months ago who hosts seminars on creativity. I came to admire some of the risks that he takes to get his points across.

Through various exercises, he gets participants to face their creative challenges and fears. For example, he makes everybody sing, whether they feel they can or not. Invariably a number of people will feel very uncomfortable and complain. A few will leave.

But he doesn't seem concerned all that much about them. He seems more interested in serving the needs of the people who stay—the ones who also feel afraid, but who are willing to work through it.

I asked him whether those who depart bother him at all.

"They used to, but I've come to appreciate something very important," he said.

"It's not for everyone! Once I saw this, I relaxed, and I accepted the rejection and carried on."

This is a tremendous insight, and it's one that we should all consider.

Where did we ever get the idea that anything, other than potable drinking water, could be good for everyone? Who told us that we have to be people-pleasers? Why are we so afraid of being rejected?

I believe it boils down to a matter of survival fear. If *everyone* rejected us, and we were exiled from civil society, cast into the wilderness, this would not be a happy outcome. Because we are at least somewhat dependent on the goodwill of others, we don't want to needlessly threaten or anger them or encourage them to lash out at us.

Notice the irrationality in this thinking. In all probability, *everyone* won't reject us, and there is no reason to believe that because a few people do so, everyone else will follow suit. Even the late Charles Manson, the convicted mass murderer, had certain admirers, and though it is hard to believe, some of them wanted to marry him.

We forget that little adage, "You can't please all of the people all of the time." To this we might add, don't even try to do it!

Scarcity thinking, the pernicious idea that there isn't enough to sustain us, leads us to believe we have to find universal acceptance. We become so solicitous of other people's high regard that we become frozen whenever someone openly disagrees with us or dislikes us.

Then, having felt the sting of rejection, we dwell on our failures and downplay our successes. This makes us recoil, and instead of reaching out as much as we can, we do the opposite, which *does* lead to failure.

One of the greatest risks of all is the attempt to avoid all risks!

Appreciate that you aren't for everyone. What should you do about it? Employ large-numbers campaigns to find and cultivate your kindred spirits, your supporters, your true peer group. By garnering more of them, you'll boost your self-confidence and will know that your detractors aren't going to have the last word.

The Telemarketers' Mistake

When you come up with something as apparently pervasive and universally applicable as the large-numbers philosophy, if you're intellectually honest, you try to brainstorm at least a few exceptions to the rule. When *doesn't* it apply? I believe I have found a significant exception.

I mentioned that I was first introduced into this kind of philosophy in my sales career. One manager cynically stated his version of it this way:

If you throw enough against the wall, some of it has to stick.

It's not a pretty image, but he got his point across.

Unfortunately, the telemarketing industry, in my estimation, perverted the Law. It has thrown so much crud at so many people so relentlessly that it is paying the price.

I'm convinced the American people are trying to put the consumer-telemarketing industry out of business. They're joining the Do Not Call Registry in droves. As of 2017, nearly 230 million numbers had been placed in this database of people who don't want to be sold over the phone when they are at home.

This legislation didn't occur overnight. It took decades of consumer abuse and outrage as well as utter stupidity and miscalculation on the part of telemarketers. Telemarketers have been at war with consumers for a long time, and there has been an escalating "arms race" that has accompanied it.

On the whole, the telemarketing industry has always operated from the assumption that "there are more of you where you came from!" It is an arrogant perversion of the Law of Large Numbers.

Telemarketers believed that if they offended some potential buyers, all they had to do was dial up other prospects and pitch them. Call enough people, the thinking went, and some of them simply had to say yes.

People responded by hanging up faster, so telemarketers spieled faster, making their offers sound both unattractive and incomprehensible.

Consumers then asserted themselves and reflexively said no to more offers. Telemarketers developed autodialers to get to the next prospect faster.

Home answering machines arrived on the scene, enabling consumers to screen the calls that came in, so telemarketers invented software to distinguish live from recorded voices.

More households had two people working by day, so telemarketers began to call more often at night, when people were at home. They swarmed the dinner hour, broadly construed as 5 to 9 p.m. This aroused even more resentment.

Other machines, called predictive dialers, were invented to hunt down people who were at home during the daytime. These machines were responsible for mysteriously hanging up on millions of people who had answered, but to whom no telemarketer was available to speak at the time.

Countless elderly and infirm people struggled to reach telephones that stopped ringing before they could arrive. Often alone in their homes, these folks said hello and were hung up on after suffering through ominous, fear-inducing seconds of silence.

And when all else failed to generate enough people to speak to, telemarketers decided to simply call everyone—that huge database known as America—more frequently.

In military parlance, think of the telemarketing strategy as a sustained carpet-bombing campaign. To use another metaphor, there were fewer fish in the pond, so telemarketers decided to fish even more often and to use howitzers to blow what fish remained out of the water. Ecology, conservation, and the careful husbanding of resources never seemed to enter the industry's consciousness. How come? Because these practices emphasize cooperation, and telemarketing has been steeped in a hostile, defensive mind-set from which it has yet to emerge.

Moreover, like the military-industrial complex that American presidents have warned of, there is a technology complex that is the financial backbone of and veritable arms dealer to the telemarketing business. Consisting of manufacturers and distributors of equipment of various kinds, including dialing and database-management technologies, this technology complex has been dedicated to making poor contacts even cheaper to make.

"Yes, your calls are terrible in quality," they might acknowledge, "but our gizmos will help you to make more of them, at a lower cost!"

In other words, *we'll help you to do even more of the wrong thing!*

Efficiency wins, but overall effectiveness loses.

Now, through the Do Not Call Registry, citizens are using the same database technologies that telemarketers developed in order to opt out of being called!

It Didn't Have to Turn Out This Way

There is a major lesson here, illustrated by my experience with a salesman I am calling Ben Terry. Ben worked for me at Time-Life Books. At twenty, I was his manager, and at sixty or so, he was one of my sales reps.

Ben was one of our best. He didn't put the largest numbers on the board. In fact, his raw sales numbers were barely in the top half. But Ben's sales were of the highest quality.

We contacted consumers and asked them to try the lead book from one of our libraries on a ten-day trial basis. If they liked it and bought it, they'd receive another book every other month on the same trial basis. They could keep the ones they liked, send back the rest, and cancel at any time.

There were two objectives for the sales rep: (1) sell the ten-day trial and (2) sell the idea of paying for the book and of looking forward to future books.

Most reps concentrated on pushing books out the door, and they benefited in part because in addition to an hourly wage, they were paid a small spiff for each confirmed trial order they wrote. They could make significantly more money if and when their prospects paid for the initial books.

Ben didn't push out large numbers, as I said. He wasn't flashy or unduly aggressive. But he was, hands down, the overall champion in encouraging the people he sold to pay for their books.

Disproportionately more of his initial buyers turned into paid accounts than anyone else's on my sales team. In a word, Ben's sales "collected," while others' returned their trial books in far greater numbers. In actual percentages, Ben collected at 45 percent and above at the time of the first billing of the customer. His peers collected at 20 percent or less.

Ben was, simply put, the best salesperson we had, but until you calculated all of the pertinent numbers, you wouldn't know this. You needed a large number of large numbers to appreciate his value. One metric, his daily production figure, wasn't enough to enable anyone to appreciate what Ben was doing for the company.

I did some math. Ben spoke to individual buyers longer than the average rep. Yet he completed more presentations and actually asked for more orders. How can that be? I'll net it out for you.

He was a great communicator.

He loved our books! He focused on selling the Library of Art, which contained over twenty volumes, ranging over centuries. To hear him describe the works of even the least-known masters was sheer poetry. You could sense from his words and tones how beautiful the textures of the photography looked.

The way Ben approached a conversation was an art in itself. Each conversation was his masterpiece. He compelled through kindness and keen interest and obvious enthusiasm.

I wondered, who *wouldn't* buy from Ben?

What did Ben do with nonbuyers? Did he angrily disconnect them, as some of his peers were known to do? Never! He wished his nos a very pleasant day or evening. Because he had been so polite, he knew that he would speak to them again in three or four months, and they might be more receptive at that point.

This insight—that if he treated people kindly and politely, he would get a chance to pitch them again and again—was Ben's brilliant application of the Law of Large Numbers.

He made a great impression on everyone—so much so that most would recognize his voice and manner when he called again. And they'd be more receptive to subsequent presentations than they were to earlier ones, not more resistant, which is usually the case with lesser salespeople.

When was the last time you remember a salesperson for being wonderful?

Ben specialized in having meaningful conversations. In these chats, customers are engaged as people. Their values are discussed or implicated, their likes and dislikes become clear. In a word, sellers and buyers bond, as Ben did with his customers.

In Zen terminology, Ben gently required a person to be utterly and completely *inside* of the conversation. You had to *be here now*. I'm sure countless meals were taken off the stove to simmer while happily immersed people chatted with Ben.

If we had some 2 million Ben Terrys on the phones, there wouldn't be a Do Not Call Registry. There would also be a lot more art lovers.

Record Breakers Are Usually Large-Numbers People

Above I spoke about surfers, and how they can wait for great periods of time before they actually catch any waves. There is one fellow, a record breaker in the world of surfing, who isn't known for the number of rides he has been able to garner. Nor is he known for the size of the waves he has caught or for the number of wipeouts he has survived. He has broken a different record entirely.

Dale Webster surfed every day for twenty-eight and a half years at a particular beach near Bodega Bay, on California's northern coast. When *Los Angeles Times* sportswriter Bill Plaschke asked him why he did it, Webster replied that he hoped to figure it out one day

According to the author of *Callings*, Gregg Levoy, "Sometimes we follow a passion just for the following, just to be close to it, with no particular end in mind."

Surfing every day for nearly three decades may not be your sort of achievement, but I'm sure that doesn't matter much to Mr. Webster. He made a decision to rack up a certain number of consecutive visits to the ocean, and he achieved it.

The Guinness Book of Large Numbers?

If look at *The Guinness Book of World Records*, you'll see that most top-ranking accomplishments have a large-numbers component to them. Someone has eaten the most hard-boiled eggs in an hour, and someone else has walked the farthest or climbed the highest mountain with the greatest frequency. Most of these endeavors can be denominated in large numbers.

Many large-numbers people are hobbyists. I'll guess that someone out there can boast about having the largest collection of salt and pepper shakers from Route 66. Others collect old 45 or 78 records. And some wealthy folks are simply happy collecting Rolls-Royces or Corvettes.

As humans, we appreciate abundance. We love growth, having the most toys, and measuring our progress. We compare ourselves to others through our acquisitions and multiple interests, financial, cultural, educational, and otherwise. Counting them comes naturally.

There's No Joy in Heaven over Empty Churches

In my ongoing effort to ferret out exceptions to this principle, I thought I had stumbled upon one. How, I asked myself, could *spirituality* have anything to do with large numbers?

Then I remembered a quote that one of my professors used in his lectures. According to my teacher, St. Augustine said, "There's no joy in heaven over empty churches." In other words, there is nothing uplifting about preaching to an empty choir.

If you think about it, isn't there more electricity and fervor in nearly any large gathering of people? In this sense, isn't the idea of a full house of worship an inspiring thing—something to be sought by anyone who supports organized religion?

Reincarnation: A Large-Numbers Concept

Speaking of spirituality, there are world religions that subscribe to the idea of reincarnation. In their view, we'll keep being reborn "until we get it right."

The *it* to which they refer is to higher consciousness. Some call it *nirvana*, and others call it *satori*. Earlier in this book, I referred to it as *enlightenment*. They're roughly interchangeable terms.

In some ways, this is a very upbeat perspective. In effect, it says that we don't have to get it all during this very brief passage we call our lives. As long as we make continuous progress, we'll wake up eventually. We get a large number of bites at the apple. Miss it now, and it will bob our way again.

What a relief! If true, we can relax, which will have the effect of heightening our consciousness, necessitating fewer trips back to the worldly realm.

Apply Large Numbers to
Your Skills Development

Most shortcomings in relationships can be traced to poor communications. If we want to cure our ailing communications, we need to do a few crucial things.

First, we need to try different ways to get our ideas across. One thing that brilliant teachers do is generate multiple examples to which individuals can relate.

If someone is a ballplayer, the instructor will use examples from his or her sport. A dancer or actor will be treated to illustrations from the performing arts. The inspiring instructor tries to reach out in multiple ways to ensure that all people in her class will identify with the material.

Most of us, on the other hand, try a "one size fits all" strategy. We don't adjust our messages to different individuals and situations. We might try something, and if it works, well, fine. If it doesn't, we give up.

When communications become less frequent, interpersonal relationships cool off and become chilly. "We never talk anymore," people explain. By not talking enough, people forget the things that they have in common.

The same principle applies to relations between countries. As long as governments are committed to communicating with each other regularly, there are heightened chances for peace and mutual betterment. This is why international organizations schedule regular meetings. When they shut down these efforts, closing off channels, wars break out.

Go Ahead—Give It Away Every Now and Then

Among other things, I teach independent consultants how to build their practices. In my seminars, I mention that accepting nonpaying assignments, such as speech engagements before local or regional associations, hasn't paid off for me, and therefore I avoid them.

But let me suggest something to you, which is also a reminder to me. If you're in a situation where you have the time, volunteering your skills can be very beneficial. I ran across an expression that seems to explain it:

You can't truly help someone else without helping yourself at the same time.

I've experienced the wisdom of this insight. The other day I donated my lunch hour to giving individual help to some seminar attendees. Time flew by, and before I knew it, all I had time to do was wolf down a roll before the general session resumed.

Instead of feeling cheated of an entitlement, I felt energized. I knew I actually helped some folks who were too shy to share their questions in front of the entire class. Moreover, I felt I made a real contribution to their development. I can't tell you how many times I've been paid to help companies where people resisted change, and I walked away wondering whether I served any of their long-term goals.

Not being paid, on an occasional basis, can actually enable you to throw yourself, your real self, into your work. Perhaps this is why so many retired folks get joy out of volunteer work.

From a large-numbers perspective, volunteering makes you busy, and when you're busy, you reach a critical mass of activity. Because you're circulating, you're being stimulated. And from this you will inevitably feel more creative, think new thoughts, and restore your vitality. Occasionally, you'll rub shoulders with another volunteer who just happens to need what you offer and who will be more than willing to pay you to provide it. By working at your side in a volunteer context, they have come to know and trust you, so bringing you into other contexts seems to be only natural.

Don't Get Too Picky

Have you ever asked yourself, "What am I saving myself for?"

I have, and it's a perfectly suitable question, especially when I've been passing up opportunities. Over the years, I've received a number of inquiries that I would respond to differently if I had the chance.

For instance, I passed up some paid speaking engagements in faraway lands. The way I figured it, between travel, performance, and jet lag, I was going to invest a week or two to get only a few days of work and compensation. Frankly, I placed no value on introducing myself to different cultures. I saw the proposals exclusively as business opportunities, and I declined them on that basis. Now, given world tensions and hostilities, it is much more dangerous to travel to these venues. It's likely that I'll never see them.

Upon self-examination, I have to say that I've over-practiced saying no and underpracticed saying yes. It's consistent with the saying, "It isn't what you do that you regret; it's what you *didn't* do."

Now I'm choosing to accept more exotic and challenging assignments, and I'm having a lot more fun.

Devise Your Own Large-Numbers Action Plan

You've had a chance to see more than a hundred examples and applications of the Law of Large numbers in these pages. I hope that they have convinced you that this principle is nearly universal. It seems to fit most situations, careers, goals, and challenges that we face.

Now it's time to put it to work. See it in action. Prove or disprove it for yourself, and please let me know how you're using it.

I suggest you start by examining your current problems and challenges. Take several minutes to list them. Don't leave any out! Put them all down.

Now that they're in front of you, ask yourself these questions:

1. How is a small-numbers mentality or habit pattern informing these problems?

2. How can I break through this difficulty, or address this problem, by adopting a large-numbers consciousness?

Finally, ask yourself, with regard to each problem:

3. What can I do right away in large numbers that will change the reality of this situation?

Let me give you a few personal examples of how I put these questions to use.

Right now, I'm devising some seminars for executives and professionals on personal safety and assault prevention. I don't have all the time in the world to invest in their development. I need to make them cost-effective right away.

The first thing I have done is to write course descriptions. Second, I have amassed some good lists of potential sponsors of the seminars. Third, I have called and emailed a large number of these potential supporters. I've also decided to follow up with the initially interested ones until they either say yes or no. Then I'll assess the desirability of rolling out a major campaign.

I'm finding that there is interest in these programs, and a university encouraged me to submit a course outline. I wrote one up, and rewrote my résumé at that university's request. As a result, it has booked one of my programs for delivery within four months. With that success in hand, I have followed up with some of my initial inquiries, and I'm about to roll out the program more widely.

Where I had originally contacted thirty or forty potential sponsors, this time I'll probably contact five to ten times as many and then perform an additional assessment. The total time I have expended in this large-numbers campaign has been less than three weeks. This gives you an idea of what you can accomplish in a short period of time.

Diversify!

I'm also using a large-numbers approach in another way. Instead of relying on one seminar to bring me success, I'm simultaneously testing three. Two seminars are spinoffs of the original. They're aimed at even larger audiences. By diversifying, I'm doing what any investment manager would do. I'm refusing to put all of my eggs into one basket. I'm also increasing the odds that at least one of my seminars will be a hit.

What Happens When You Have a Hit on Your Hands?

What will I do when one of my ships comes in?

Certainly I'll concentrate my resources on exploiting it. That's only logical.

Yet at the same time, I absolutely must avoid the mistake of concentrating on it so much that I forget to test newer and better topics. A large-numbers commitment means that you never stop deploying your assets. If you do, you'll invite greater risks, and promote the scarcity that none of us wants.

Let me give you an example, again from my experience. At various times as a consultant, I've endeavored to fill my schedule with paying work. On the surface, that seems to be a rational goal. After all, it's better to be paid for your time than to be squandering it, right?

But I've always found that maximizing my billable days has necessitated that I curtail the number of companies for which I consult. In other words, if I want to be busy all the time, it requires that *fewer* clients buy more time from me. Instead of continuously marketing, I get lazy, and think that these few organizations will always be there to support me, and frankly that is unrealistic. What happens in actual fact is that I paint myself into a corner and pay the price later on when I have to hustle for larger numbers of clients.

It's just a better idea to *always* have large-numbers campaigns going on in every significant area of your personal and professional life.

What Kind of Person Will You Become?

I hope that you'll take the ideas in this book and put them to work everywhere. I also think that one of the greatest things that can happen is to see what a large-numbers mentality will mean to you as a person.

I believe you'll become more confident, because you'll understand what it takes to succeed in any area.

I believe you'll feel more willing and able to pay the price of achieving victory.

I believe you'll come to appreciate that failure is temporary, and that it is simply a matter of judging your performance before you have had a chance to rack up more victories.

I believe that when you give yourself enough time, you'll find you can master anything, whether it is a martial art, or as we have seen, passing the toughest bar examination in the country after forty-eight attempts.

I believe you'll come to see that your destiny is in your own hands. You might enter a field and learn that the odds of excelling are low, but that field has never encountered *you* before! By your own commitment, your own hard work and dedication, you'll shift those odds in your favor.

I believe you'll become a more relaxed, less distressed individual, because you won't doubt whether your goals are attainable. You'll calmly accept the fact that they are.

I believe you'll come to see that a major difference in the attitudes of people boils down to whether they are small- or large-numbers practitioners.

Do they believe that the basic condition of the universe is one of scarcity or abundance?

Do they take for granted the idea that they are only given so many opportunities, or that they create their own opportunities?

Do they think that the purpose of life is to expand their powers or to fit into the pigeonholes that other people assign to them?

Do they think that their choices diminish as they mature, or that they grow?

Fundamentally, are they at cause, believing that they are the prime movers of their lives, or are they at effect? Do they think that every hope, dream, and aspiration is controlled by others, or determined by chance or whim?

Most people suffer from these delusions, but you won't when you put the Law to work in your life. But be prepared to meet some resistance, some detractors. Some people will look at you and think you're mad or bad because you have upgraded your ambitions. I can't tell you how many people think there must be something wrong with me because I have earned five college degrees (and frankly, I may go back for more!).

They fail to see that it is not desirable to settle for less education when you can have more. Our society's fundamental strength resides in, among other things, its system of higher education. No one is stopping us from learning as much as we can for as long as we can. It was Plato or Aristotle who said that learning is one of the few goods that it is impossible to have too much of.

So be on alert. Safeguard your large-numbers philosophy, and if necessary, don't disclose it to potential detractors. Just put it to work and enjoy the results you reap, results that will induce lesser folks to wonder, "Where did *that* come from?"

Afterword

I enjoyed writing this book. It has special significance for me, because at the basis of all of my success, I can see the large-numbers philosophy in operation.

I hope that you have become extraordinarily successful by employing it.

Please let me know how you're doing.

Dr. Gary S. Goodman
(818) 970-GARY (4279)
drgaryscottgoodman@yahoo.com
gary@drgarygoodman.com
gary@customersatisfaction.com

Printed in the USA
CPSIA information can be obtained
at www.ICGtesting.com
JSHW012038140824
68134JS00033B/3135